AN
UNFORESEEN
LIFE

A MEMOIR

BY
MARY ANN CONNELL

ISBN: 978-1-936946-79-2

The Nautilus Publishing Company
426 S Lamar Blvd., Suite 16
Oxford, MS 38655
Tel: 662-513-0159
www.nautiluspublishing.com

First Edition

Front cover design by Carroll Chiles Moore
Interior design by Sinclair Rishel

Library of Congress Cataloging-in-Publication Data has been applied for.

Printed in Canada

10 9 8 7 6 5 4 3 2 1

William Augustus Strong, Jr. and
Mary Emma Danzey Strong, circa 1963

For my mother and father

I asked God for strength, that I might achieve,

I was made weak, that I might learn humbly to obey…

I asked for health, that I might do greater things,

I was given infirmity, that I might do better things…

I asked for riches, that I might be happy,

I was given poverty, that I might be wise…

I asked for power, that I might have the praise of men,

I was given weakness, that I might feel the need of God…

I asked for all things, that I might enjoy life,

I was given life, that I might enjoy all things…

I got nothing that I asked for – but everything I had hoped for,

Almost despite myself, my unspoken prayers were answered.

I am among all people, most richly blessed.

Preface

Saturday, November 3, 1945

M y five-year-old brother, Billy, stood with his hands on his hips. He was dressed in his cowboy costume.

"We'll get in trouble if we play with matches," he said, tentatively.

Billy may not have thought it was a good idea, but I did. Our mother had traveled to Pensacola to attend her sister Belle's funeral. Our father was stationed on Guam. Miss Maude White, a teacher in our schools, and Ruby Dee, our teenaged babysitter, were keeping us. They were both inside.

Billy and I gathered rocks from the back of our yard and carried them under several big oak and pecan trees. We stacked the rocks in a circle and then put two more layers of rocks on top to form a wall around what would be our campfire. We raked leaves, which were in abundance in our wooded yard in early November, placed them inside the stone circle, and threw some sticks on top.

I remembered there was a box of matches in the kitchen. When I went into the house, neither Miss White nor Ruby Dee saw me. I slipped the box of matches under my vest and walked back out to our campfire site.

I struck the first match and held it next to the dry leaves. They instantly caught fire. The fire blazed much higher than I had anticipated. I climbed over the rock wall surrounding the fire to retrieve a long stick we were going to use to poke the fire. My foot got caught between two of the rocks in the wall, and I could not get my foot free.

Billy climbed over the wall to help me get out when a spark from the fire set his furry chaps ablaze. There was a roaring sound. Within seconds, fire was all over Billy.

He started running. He screamed. In terrible pain.

I didn't know what to do, so I chased him and screamed in terror.

I chased Billy around the side yard and then across our front yard. The faster Billy ran, the faster the flames engulfed him.

I
Louisville, Mississippi

1

My father was in trial in the Circuit Court of Winston County, Mississippi. The court recessed when he was called home to await the birth of his first child.

As my father left the courthouse, he told the judge and clerks that he would signal the arrival of the baby by sending up a smoke signal.

"White smoke," he said, "if the baby is a girl. Black smoke," he continued, "if it is a boy."

Louisville had no hospital. My mother had a miscarriage with twins in 1936, so Dr. Bernard Hickman and his wife, Florence, a nurse — close, personal friends of my parents — came to her side at the first hint of labor. They said they would stay with my mother until the child was delivered.

Word spread around Louisville of my pending birth and of the signaling method.

At 8:20 a.m., on the morning of October 12, 1937, Dr. Hickman held me up — a healthy baby girl. Florence prepared me for my mother to hold.

My father rushed to the living room to lay the fire. He piled it high with oak. White smoke rose from the chimney at our home on Park Street.

My father insisted I be named Mary in honor of my mother. I am not sure how they decided on Ann or the use of a double name, but Mary Ann it has been from that day on.

Through the years my parents told me what a good baby I was. I was always on schedule and cried little. They raised me in accord with a pamphlet provided by the U.S. government. During the 1930s, many experts decided that raising children was like running a factory — everything should run on time. Government pamphlets suggested that feeding, bedtime, and exercise should be on a schedule as regular as clockwork. My mother adhered to the government pamphlet, which also emphasized that once the baby was put to bed, she was to be left alone.

Two years passed and my brother, William Augustus Strong, III (Billy) was born on October 4, 1939. The Hickmans, again, were at my parents' side as he came into the world. My father billowed black smoke, signaling to the community that Billy had arrived.

My parents raised Billy by the government book too. He was kept to a rigid schedule, but Billy had a sweeter disposition than I did. He was more affectionate and loving. He adored my mother, and me and told us frequently how beautiful we were and how he loved to hear my mother sing "Billy Boy, Billy Boy, Oh, Where Have You Been, Charming Billy?"

One day, when Billy and I were playing in the front yard, a young black girl walking down the sidewalk stopped and spoke to my mother.

"I am looking for work," she said. "I can help care for children."

"How old are you?" my mother asked, believing the girl couldn't be older than ten.

"Thirteen," she lied, "but I know how to take care of children and need the work."

This is how Ruby Dee Eiland came to work for our family.

Ruby Dee was actually nine.

Ruby Dee regularly took us one block down the street to "The Little Park." We played with Sylvia Duck, Edward Lee Prisock, Jimmy Turner, and Betty Jean Davis… and their caregivers. Some of my fondest memories are of the times we had swinging, sliding down the big slide, and chasing each other in the park. On special days, after a day of play, Jimmy's mother would serve us cherry pie. Interestingly, Jimmy's caregiver's name was "Cherry."

We lived across the street from Mr. and Mrs. Deck Fair. We called Mrs. Fair "Aunt Belle." She always welcomed the neighborhood children and served us cookies. She and my grandmother, Hassie Strong, were close friends. They took trips together, always chauffeured by Malcolm in Aunt Belle's large, black limousine.

Our home was beautiful, especially when it was decorated at Christmas (my favorite decorations were the candleholders with blue electric candle lights in the windows of the living room). On Christmas Eve, we would ride three blocks downtown to Main Street to see the lights and decorations.

Among my most vivid memories of life on Park Street was of the 1940 big snowstorm, producing snow that came up to my waist. My mother took pictures of Billy and me after the storm.

The *Winston County Journal* was published once a week in Louisville. Citizens of the community eagerly awaited its arrival on Friday afternoons. The *Journal* covered all social events in the community regardless of size. My mother loved to throw birthday parties for Billy and me. The *Journal* reported that my mother "entertained at a lovely birthday party for her little daughter, Mary Ann, on the anniversary of her first birthday."

The birthday tradition carried on and then swelled in the years to come. In 1941, the *Journal* reported that "in celebration of her fourth birthday anniversary, little Mary Ann Strong was honored with a colorful birthday party at the home of her parents, Attorney and Mrs. W.A. Strong, Jr., on Park Street." The guest list had now increased to 50 children and numerous high school helpers, plus my mother's friends, who helped serve ice cream, cake, and punch.

When my parents added a Shetland pony ride, it took our birthdays celebrations to a new high.

I loved our home and our neighbors. I was doted on by my parents and grandparents (and Ruby Dee picked up when they weren't around). The neighborhood children, for the most part, were kind and always seemed happy to see me.

And, of course, there was my little brother Billy. He was a sweet, generous child, and he adored me. He couldn't pronounce *Mary Ann*. He called me *May Ran*. Much to my delight, Billy followed me everywhere. When he couldn't keep up, he would call out, "*May Ran*! Wait for me!"

Life for me in Louisville, Mississippi was uncluttered, simple.

2

In October of 1943, Billy and I tacked a nail into the woodwork on the front door to our home on South Columbus Avenue. We hung the service flag, approved by the U.S. Congress, to display at the homes of anyone serving in the military of the United States during the war. The service flag was 8" by 5 ¼" with a red border, white center, and a blue star in the middle for each service member living and a gold star for each family member who had died during military service. Our father had just enlisted.

My father had tried to volunteer for service as soon as the Japanese attacked Pearl Harbor, but he was rejected by every military branch. He was 35 years old. His sense of patriotism and loyalty drove him to continue to try to enlist until finally, in late 1943, he was accepted into the Navy's Seabees program. The work of the Seabees — a division of the Navy that constructs roads, bridges, and airfields — was physically demanding and designed for younger, stronger men.

He was first assigned to Camp Perry in Williamsburg, Virginia, and served there as a librarian for several months. From there, he traveled by train to Camp Parks, California. During his travels, he wrote my mother, Billy, and me letters describing the terrain of the plains, the Rocky Mountains, and the boredom of the long rides. In one of the letters, my father described a craps game. One of the men on board stole money from another service man. My father lent the gentleman his last bit of money so his new friend could continue participating in the game.

While my father was stationed at Camp Parks, my mother took Billy and me twice to see him. On one of the trips, Peggy Jean Boydstun and her mother went with us because her father was also stationed nearby in California.

Through the war years, like so many other children, Billy and I collected scrap newspaper and metal and took them to the scrap bins where the gov-

Mary Ann and Billy, circa 1944

ernment recycled these items to make military supplies. We put our small savings into war bonds. We felt like we were contributing to the war effort.

Butter, sugar, and chocolate were rationed. Everyone was required to register for war ration books, which provided the stamps we used to buy tires, food, and gas. It took the combined stamps of both the Strong and Boydstun families, plus help from friends in Louisville, to allow us to make the trips across the country to see our fathers.

The miles were long and tiring in a car with no air conditioning. There was constant worry about where we would stay. We rarely passed a motel, but when we did, "No Vacancy" signs were usually posted. When there were "Vacancy" signs, the motels were often not habitable. One night, somewhere in New Mexico or Arizona, we finally found a place with a "Vacancy" sign and checked in to find the room and bath so filthy that we could not stay. We left in the middle of the night and drove on.

As we approached military bases, we passed dozens of young servicemen hitchhiking to the nearest town. We always picked one up and gave him a ride. We never gave a thought to our safety because these boys were wearing sailor uniforms just like my father.

One particular young man had a roll of string and a pack of notebook paper. He helped us make signs with all sorts of messages on them, tie them to the strings, hang them out the back car windows, and watch them float in the breeze until a car would come along and run over our message system.

Billy and I had marine uniforms. We were proud to wear royal blue and gold and had our pictures taken in them to send to my father.

Eventually, my father was shipped to Guam, an island in the Pacific 6,000 miles west of San Francisco and 1,500 miles south of Tokyo, where he helped build runways, one of the most dangerous duties on the Pacific islands. He also protected the engineers and construction workers from Japanese snipers hiding in the caves overlooking the runways. He sent Billy a letter opener made with a base from a bullet casing and a blade, roughhewn by hand, with Billy's name on it. He sent home another one for himself with his name on it. "Guam" was etched on both of them.

Even though he had a law degree, my father was never promoted to officer. This bothered him. The rationale was that he had not graduated from college. My father had attended both Vanderbilt University in Nashville, Tennessee, and Union University in Jackson, Tennessee, before going to law school at Cumberland University in Lebanon, Tennessee, but he did not technically graduate from college. In those days, an undergraduate degree was not required to enter law school.

As a result, my father worked as a Seabee alongside other young enlisted men mostly in their late teens or early 20s. By this time, he was 38.

Eventually, he was asked to represent sailors who were court-martialed and did an excellent job of providing legal representation for them. One of his commanding officers wrote: "Strong made a very thorough investigation of the case and of the points of law involved. He prepared an excellent defense for the accused. His position as an enlisted man appearing before a General Court-Martial was a bit unusual. He conducted himself with dignity and with great credit for his legal ability."

3

My sweet brother Billy was slender, black-haired, and looked much like my father.

Billy entered first grade in the fall of 1945. He did well in school and seemed to like it. He also worked diligently on the good manners my mother insisted upon. When she had a dinner party for me on my 8th birthday, I wore a long dress my grandmother Strong made for me. Billy wore dark blue slacks, a sport coat, and a white shirt and tie.

My mother set the dining room table with her best china and silver. She had taught Billy how to pull the chair out for her... and then for me. After we were seated, Billy would sit down, put his napkin in his lap and, wait for Mother to ask the blessing. He knew not to pick up his knife or fork to begin eating until my mother had lifted her own fork. Billy did everything she had taught him to do and, he was quite pleased with himself and his good table manners.

Billy loved to please both my mother and me.

As in most Southern towns, Saturday afternoon matinées were the best times of the week. Mother gave us ten cents each to go to the "picture show" to see the Saturday afternoon cowboy films. My favorite was Roy Rogers and his horse, Trigger. The main feature was always preceded by a serial that was thrilling and left me waiting anxiously for the next week to see whether Tiger Woman would fall into the boiling cauldron of hot oil or be saved at the last minute from her disastrous fate.

Ruby Dee always accompanied us to the movie, but she had to sit in the balcony with the other colored people of Louisville.

The Saturday afternoon picture show began at 1:30 and ended around 3:30. After the movie on Saturday, November 3, 1945, we all walked home, which took about fifteen minutes. I had worn my cowgirl outfit, which had a skirt, vest, and a play gun and holster. Billy wore his cowboy outfit.

We talked on the way home about how the real cowboys also wore chaps with their cowboy clothes. Billy wanted to put on his chaps so he would look just like the cowboys in the show.

After Billy tied his chaps to his pants legs, we went outside to play.

"Let's build a fire like they did in the show," I said.

"We'll get in trouble if we play with matches," he said tentatively.

Mary Ann and Billy, circa 1945

4

The faster Billy ran, the faster the flames engulfed him.

Our neighbors, Ruth and Dr. Charlie Blue, who were walking down the street in front of our house, saw what was happening, and came running to help. By then, Mrs. Watson from next door heard the screams and came running too. She grabbed Billy and rolled him over and over in the dirt until she at last squelched the last of the flames. She was burned terribly over her arms and body.

Billy never stopped screaming in pain.

Mrs. Watson, the Blues, Miss White, and Ruby Dee were all in the front yard by then. They took Billy into the entrance hall of our home and called for an ambulance.

It seemed to take forever for the ambulance to arrive.

Billy stood next to a blue chair in the entrance hall. Billy's screams never stopped.

"May Ran," he screamed over and over to me, "I'm going to die. Help me."

He jumped up and down and then cried, "I'm freezing."

I ran upstairs and brought him the new bathrobe my mother had given me for my birthday three weeks earlier. I put it around his shoulders. All Billy's clothing had burned into his body, except for his face and eyes.

The ambulance finally arrived, and they took Billy away.

And then, I was sent to spend the night at my friend Cin Robertson's house.

My mother arrived in Louisville shortly after midnight — a few minutes before Billy died.

The next morning, my Strong grandparents came for me. They walked into the bedroom. My friend Cin left the room.

My grandmother sat on the side of my bed and held my hand.

"Mary Ann," my grandmother told me, "Billy has gone to heaven to live with God."

I buried my head in the pillow and cried.

Within a day, Senator Eastland's office arranged for my father to leave Guam. But in the rush to gain discharge approval, no one arranged for transportation back home.

My father tried everything, but the war was ending. Hundreds of thousands of military personnel were vying for every seat on every airplane. He simply could not obtain transportation.

Finally, in an act of desperation, my father stowed away in the tail gun area of a military transport plane. He was discovered by an officer doing inspection. He explained his frantic need to get home, but the officer had no sympathy.

"Get off, or I will have you court-martialed," the officer told him.

My father got off the plane and stood by the runway. He watched his only hope to get home take off at sunset over the Pacific.

He thought about his wife and daughter alone in the States, and the son he would never see again. As he watched the airplane bank to the right, it exploded in mid-air.

Everyone on board was killed.

5

When it was clear my father would not be coming home, my mother decided to move ahead with Billy's funeral. The custom in Louisville was to place the body of a deceased person in his casket in the home, not at a funeral home.

Billy was placed in our living room. He was dressed in the dark blue pants, coat, and tie that he had worn at my eighth birthday party.

During the two nights before the funeral, I would slip quietly down the stairs to look at Billy. I talked to him. I wanted him back.

I did not want anyone to see me cry. The only time I did was when I slipped downstairs and looked at Billy in his casket.

The funeral was held at the Methodist church in Louisville. Marjorie Woodruff, a local soloist, sang "Sweetest Little Fellow, Mighty Like a Rose."

The funeral and burial were a blur for me. In the days that followed, I spent hours collecting the remnants of the many floral arrangements that were sent. I took them out to the site of the campfire and arranged them and then rearranged them.

All I wanted was to have Billy back. I am ashamed to admit that I did not consider what my mother was going through at the time. All I thought about was me — and the horrible images of Billy screaming with pain, his clothes burning deep into his body.

A family friend and local attorney, Hoy Hathorn, drove his car up to our front door. A passenger got out, but I did not recognize him.

It was my father returning from war. Gone was his beautiful black hair, replaced with gray.

I was glad to have my father home, but our home now was quiet and sad.

A few days after his return, I crept up the stairs to my room. I overheard my parents talking in their room.

"Why in the world would Mary Ann have gotten matches and started a fire?" my father asked. "She knew better," he added.

I had believed Billy's death was my fault. Overhearing my parents' conversation, I knew it was true.

The guilt of Billy's death weighed on me every day. Even at the age of eight, I understood that I needed to make things right. With God. With my parents. With the world.

I worked hard to excel in all my endeavors.

I went to church on Sunday mornings and Wednesday nights.

I sang in the choir.

I practiced the piano.

I practiced the saxophone.

I studied.

My carefree days had come to an end.

II

My Childhood After Billy

Mary Ann, circa 1947

6

By the time I was in fourth grade, I had learned to play the alto saxophone well enough to perform a solo for my class.

These were the moments I worked toward. A moment of glory. A moment to make up for my actions.

I had practiced endlessly and chose to play "The Old Lamplighter."

Soon after I began to play, our teacher, Mrs. Legan, stopped me.

"Mary Ann," she said, "Let me interrupt you for a moment."

She walked over to the classroom door and escorted a new freckled-face boy into the room.

"Class," she said, "I'd like to introduce your new classmate, E. Grady Jolly, who has recently moved here from Columbus, Mississippi."

I was furious my solo was interrupted. Nonetheless, I smiled, minding my manners, with the hope Mrs. Legan would seat him in the back of the room and I could continue my performance.

But Mrs. Legan seated this new boy in a vacant seat on Row 2, directly behind my desk. Then, she told me to continue.

I was unnerved by the interruption; however, I picked up my saxophone and began again with my performance of a tune about an old man making his way up and down the street lighting the street lamps at night fall.

At the melodic arc in the song, I squeaked with a loud and piercing noise. I was humiliated.

The new boy in class brazenly started laughing, pumping his head up and down on the desk, making fun of me. He continued to snicker and make fun of me for the "squeaking" sound I had made.

I was determined never to speak to him again.

My anger gradually subsided as he and I became friends and spent hours in each other's homes. I adored his parents, Mr. and Mrs. Jolly, and his sister, Mary Ann Jolly. They were a family-oriented group and accepted me into their home with kindness and love. They frequently took me with them to the family night dinners at the First Presbyterian Church. I remember the caramel cake that someone brought. I would start my place in line at the dessert end to get a piece of that cake before moving back to the casseroles and fried chicken.

Life in Louisville was simple. I walked to school and rode my bike to all after-school activities. We had telephones with central telephone operators (we affectionately called them "Central"). When I placed a call, Central would frequently respond with statements, such as, *Mary Ann, stop calling your mother at work. She is busy and later she is going to have her hair done.*

I frequently called my best friends, Jane and Julia Boren, only to be told by Central, *Jane and Julia have gone to play with Cin.*

The Methodists in Louisville tried to rush through the 11:00 o'clock church service on Sunday mornings to beat the Baptists to the Woodard Hotel for Sunday lunch. In the summer, I attended every church Bible School in town.

When I was ten years old, I was attending Bible School at the Baptist Church and, while browsing through some of the books in one of the rooms, I saw a prayer in a Sunday School book that captured my heart. I tore the prayer out of the book. I folded it and placed it in my purse.

Everyone in Louisville went to the movies as often as possible. Admission was ten cents. The biggest movie of this era was "Gone with the Wind." The Strand Movie Theatre broke with tradition in Louisville and showed this film on a Sunday afternoon to a packed house. I stood in line with my friends. Across Church Street, sitting in folded chairs, were several ladies from the First Baptist Church, who were taking down the names of the children (and adults) who were sinning by going to a movie on a Sunday. That evening at the Baptist Church, the preacher read the names (including mine) of those who had attended the film that afternoon and asked the church congregation to join him in a special prayer asking God to forgive us for our sinful conduct.

My beloved saxophone continued to be a part of my life and stayed in the mix of my and E. Grady's friendship. One day in the 7th grade, E. Grady and I were walking home from school.

"Put that saxophone down," he said, "I will carry it for you."

I did, and E. Grady carried it about 30 feet. Then he put it down.

"This thing is too heavy," he said. "You need to carry it yourself."

E. Grady and I were both good students, driven in our studies. We both participated in a debate in the seventh grade on the subject of whether wiretapping should be permitted. My partner and I argued that wiretapping should be allowed by public officers in emergency situations to protect our nation's security. We used an example of an American ship crossing the ocean with thousands of sailors on board when a public officer learned through wiretapping that the enemy was planning to torpedo the ship at a certain time and point. We posited the question: *Should our officer have to remain silent and not inform the captain of the ship because he had learned this information by tapping without a court order the phone of the enemy?*

Our opponents were E. Grady and Phil Snow.

We all learned much about wiretapping, working together as a team, and learning to speak in public. One of the most challenging things about our debate was having to switch sides and be prepared to argue either position.

E. Grady was much better at that than I.

My friendship with E. Grady continued to be a central part of my life. In eighth grade, he was elected "Mr. 8th Grade" and I was selected "Miss 8th Grade."

As we moved through junior high school, E. Grady and I continued our friendship, as well as our friendly competition. We learned to dance to music played on our 45 RPM records, such as "I'm Looking Over a Four Leaf Clover," "Earth Angel," "Three Coins in a Fountain," and "In the Chapel in the Moonlight."

Stanley and Jimmy Hathorn were our neighbors. We spent a lot of time shooting basketballs in our back yard. One afternoon Stanley came over with a new BB-gun he had received for his birthday. He started shooting

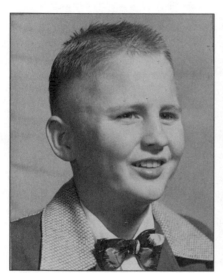 

E. Grady Jolly and Mary Ann, Mr. and Miss 8th Grade, circa 1950

sparrows perched on the power lines. I was enraged that he would shoot helpless birds and told him to stop. He paid no attention to me and kept shooting.

I ripped the gun from his arms and pointed it directly at him.

"If you ever shoot another bird on my parents' property," I shouted, "I will shoot your eyes out."

Fortunately, at that very moment, my father arrived home for lunch. He seized the gun from me and told Stanley to go home. My father added that he could not shoot birds in our yard again.

M y parents exchanged our home on South Columbus Avenue for an apartment house on East Main Street owned by Margaret and Charles Fair. I was sad to leave our beautiful home, but the memories of Billy's death there were too overwhelming for my parents.

My junior high and high school years were spent in the apartment house, and they were glorious ones. There were four apartments in the complex. We lived in one; Davis and Jen Fair lived in the one next to ours. Their first child, Dave, was born there. My parents kept one of the units for my friends and me to use for Friday night gatherings and overnight spend-the-night parties.

One cold night in the winter of 1951, the apartment house where we were living caught on fire. The firemen could not get the water hydrant to turn on because the pipes were frozen and resisted their efforts to unstick them. Hoy Hathorn, Stanley and Jimmy's father, was a short but powerful man, who was able to tug and twist the hydrant until he freed it, which enabled the firemen to pour water onto our house and save as much as they could. I remember running in and out of the house trying to retrieve as much as I could until the firemen stopped me. It was a helpless and sad feeling to stand on that freezing cold evening and watch much of what we owned destroyed by flames. It brought back terrible memories of Billy's death.

During the years that we lived in the apartment house on East Main Street, I went with my father to a political rally in front of the courthouse. I met a tall, lanky, friendly boy from Lambert, Mississippi — Jimmy Walker. We took an immediate liking to each other. He was a couple of years older than I and was already a student at Ole Miss. I had no idea at the time how important he would become in my life.

I continued to play the piano and received superior marks at the state piano festival at Belhaven College in Jackson, Mississippi. Dr. Mark Hoffman, a music professor at Ole Miss, offered me a scholarship in piano based on my receiving a superior for my playing of Chopin. I was wise enough not to accept the scholarship because I was not good enough to be a piano major.

On the evening before my high school graduation, Julia Boren and I were to present a recital. Margaret McLelland, our piano teacher and a graduate of the Cincinnati Conservatory, announced to the *Journal* that "two of Louisville's best piano students will be presented in a recital at the Louisville High School auditorium at 8:00 p.m. on Thursday, May 19, 1955." I played among my numbers a Beethoven sonata and a Debussy number. Julia played Haydn's Sonata in D Major and Rachmaninoff's Polichinelle. Together, Julia and I were to play a duo D Minor Concerto by MacDowell. I played first piano; Julia second.

About half way through the piece, I went blank and could not remember what to play next. I looked at Julia with panic in my eyes and said, "Chords." Julia understood and began to play chords while I aimlessly wandered on the keyboard up and down within the chords until, miraculously, my memory returned and I nodded at Julia that I was ready to begin where we had left off. After this less than spectacular finish, I am not sure that Mrs. McLelland would describe me again as one of "Louisville's best piano students."

In high school, extracurricular activities consumed my free time. I was editor of the *Louisville High School Review* and was elected president of the Mississippi Scholastic Press Association. After three years on the student council, I wanted to run for president of the student body, but a girl had never done that. I talked with our superintendent about the wisdom of running against Stanley Hathorn and Doug Sullivan, two very popular boys. He encouraged me to do so and not to be shy about talking about the activities in which I had been involved and the leadership positions I had held. He taught me a lesson I have never forgotten.

"Remember, Mary Ann," he said, "you can do anything you want to do if you are willing to work hard at it. Being a girl is no excuse for not reaching for your goals."

I listened to him, ran against the two boys, and was elected president by the student body. I was Homecoming Queen, Miss Louisville High School, a member of the Louisville High School Hall of Fame, a cheerleader, and commencement speaker at graduation.

But with every accomplishment, every award, there was still an empty spot inside of me. I missed my brother, Billy. And I knew deep down that his death was my fault.

High school days ended, but another era was about to begin – the era of Ole Miss. I never could have predicted, at that time, how important my college years would be in formulating my life.

III
The Ole Miss Years (1955-1959)

7

I had planned to attend Randolf Macon Woman's College in Lynchburg, Virginia, because a number of my summer camp friends were going there. When I began to think about how separated I would be from my parents and how separated they would be from me, I rethought the matter and turned my attention to Ole Miss. As an only child, I wanted my parents to know my friends and be involved in my college experience.

Through a connection I had with Betty Doty from Tupelo, I met her sister, Mary Ann Doty, who was planning to enter Ole Miss as a freshman. We decided to room together. We were assigned a room at the top of the stairs on the third floor of Ward Hall.

My mother and I traveled to Memphis in August, stayed at the Parkview Hotel next to Overton Park, and spent two days shopping for my college clothes. We had the best time together. When we returned home, I modeled all of my new clothes for my father until he must have lost his mind listening to the details of where my mother and I bought each piece and exactly what functions and where I would wear my new dresses, hats, and shoes. My mother loved clothes and fashion and enjoyed every minute of our shopping expedition. My father, while not captivated by the details of the clothes, took pleasure in seeing how happy all of this made my mother because this was a new experience for her too.

In mid-September, 1955, my parents loaded their brown and tan '98 Oldsmobile and drove me to Oxford. We were all a bit nervous and afraid. And I could tell my parents were sad that I was leaving home.

We crossed the bridge on University Avenue that spans Hilgard Cut and the train track. As we drove onto campus we were hailed down by a friendly blond-haired boy. He was wearing a shirt printed with "Welcome to Ole Miss" and "Do you need help moving in?" His name was Jimmy Rousey. He was from Laurel, Mississippi. His warm personality and radiant smile made my parents and me feel more comfortable as I embarked on this new journey.

We arrived at Ward Hall and started unloading the car. I was embarrassed by how many clothes and unnecessary items I'd packed. We made dozens of trips up and down the stairs in Ward. When it came time to unload the white stuffed teddy bear I loved and called "the Admiral" because Johnny Sharp had given it to me after attending June Week with him at the Naval Academy, my father had had enough.

"I'm not going to walk up three flights of stairs carrying a teddy bear."

Mary Ann, my roommate, arrived with her mother. They unpacked her things. Once we were both settled into our room, our parents told us goodbye and left.

Mary Ann and I walked together to the window that overlooked the front entrance of the dorm and Fulton Chapel, and watched them walk away. We waved one last goodbye.

Mary Ann and I immediately made friends on our floor. We also learned the rules of the dorm. We had to be checked into the dorm by 8:30 p.m. during the week and by 11:30 p.m. on weekends. No boys were allowed inside beyond the living room. There was one phone on each floor, and we were expected to limit our telephone calls to five minutes.

I was assigned to a freshman English class taught by one of the finest professors I had at Ole Miss – Dr. John Pilkington. Julius Collum from Jackson was in the class. He asked me to attend my first Ole Miss football game and sent me a corsage to wear to the game with the words on the card: "To the first of many good times." All the girls on the third floor of Ward thought Julius's gift was the most romantic thing they had ever seen.

8

When I was contemplating attending Ole Miss for college, I became aware, for the first time, of what a sorority was and how significant being in one was in the life of an Ole Miss student. My mother was not in a sorority and had little appreciation of its importance except through her niece, my first cousin, Jane Self, who was a Tri Delta at the University of Alabama. A number of my mother's friends in Louisville began to talk with her about sororities, mainly Tri Delta, and offered to write letters of recommendation for me to their various groups.

Ann McIntyre, a favorite friend of my mother, was a Phi Mu at Ole Miss. She invited me to visit for a weekend. I enjoyed being with the girls in the Phi Mu house. Then a Delta Gamma invited me to spend a weekend at their house, which was beautiful. The girls were friendly and welcoming. Margaret Fair recommended me for Chi Omega, and Helen Bennett recommended me for Tri Delta.

The first week of school, we launched into rush week. The sororities invited girls to a series of parties, after which they cut the list of invitees to the next round. After the final round of parties, the rushees listed their preferences and waited to see if any of the groups the girls listed invited them for membership.

During Rush Week, Mary Ann Mobley, from Brandon, Mississippi, and I had become friends and went to many of the parties together. When the last round of preferential parties were held, we chose the same three to attend. We went to Fulton Chapel together, where we were handed a card to list our preferences. We sat together as we made our final decisions. We both thought we were going to be given bids from Tri Delta, Chi Omega, and Delta Gamma, which were our three choices. Our dilemma was which one to put first.

We vacillated back and forth until we were the only two rushees left in Fulton Chapel. We made an oath to stay together. I was pulled toward Chi Omega out of respect and affection I had developed for Bess Moore from Jackson, Mississippi. Also, I was dating Julius Collum from Jackson, and he was pressuring me to join Chi Omega. Mary Ann had gained regard and friendship for Fannie Brumfield from Inverness, Mississippi. Mary Ann and I finally chose Chi Omega and returned to our respective dorms. We both received Chi Omega bids and soon became part of an 18-woman pledge class.

I feared my mother and my cousin Jane would be disappointed that I would not be a Tri Delta, but I also knew they would respect my decision.

When I returned to my dorm room in Ward Hall, I heard a young woman crying. She was talking on the phone to her father.

"Daddy," she said, in tears, "no one wanted me."

My heart broke for her.

The excitement of bid night was suddenly not so exciting.

9

We had a great group on our floor at Ward (Vonda Freeman, Betsy Beall, Elizabeth Justice, and Pat Hume). We all liked each other and got along well. In fact, we had so much fun together I earned my first "disciplinary campus."

The crime for which I was convicted by the Women's Student Government Association was for "too many girls in room and too much noise."

My punishment: for two nights I received a social restriction and could not go out at all.

One weekend in October 1955, Janis Mitchell and several other girls from Corinth were spending the weekend on the third floor of Ward. Janis was my guest. When she returned on time to the dorm from her date and attempted to sign in next to my name as her hostess, someone else had already signed in on that line. She asked the housemother what she should do and was told to go on upstairs and the matter would get sorted out in the morning. In the meantime, the girl who had signed in as my guest realized her mistake and came down and erased her name as my guest, thus leaving a blank which indicated that my guest had not come in or signed in.

The mistake was not cleared up, which resulted in my receiving another disciplinary campus.

Dr. Allen Cabaniss taught western civilization our freshman year. I loved the class and had an "A" going into the final exam my second semester.

Some kind of pill that would keep you from going to sleep was sweeping the campus at that time. I did not drink and had never taken any kind of pill that could remotely be considered a "drug." However, I was so determined to make an A+ on the final that I took one of the pills and stayed

Mrs. Rhyne, Mary Ann, and Carlene Myers, circa 1958

up for two days and nights studying for the exam. When I started writing my exam paper in the "blue book," I knew something was wrong. I found myself writing about swimming at Choctaw Lake, going to dances in Philadelphia, and all sorts of things that had nothing to do with Louis XIV, the French Revolution, or anything else Dr. Cabaniss had taught me that semester. I received my grade for the semester —"C" —. Dr. Cabaniss wrote on the cover of my blue book.

"What in the world happened to you?"

I was humiliated and ashamed of my behavior and my grade, especially since E. Grady made an "A" and was not shy about telling everyone.

Dr. Pilkington was a magnificent teacher. All the students in our freshman English class were good students. He reminded me on a number of occasions how nervous he was when he walked into our class as a relatively new Ph.D. from Harvard. He was trying to incite a class discussion on something that had to do with George Gershwin. No one was cooperating with him, and he was getting frustrated. Realizing his predicament, I asked a question about "Rhapsody in Blue" and "An American in Paris" that broke the log-jam. A lively discussion then ensued, and I knew at that moment the friendship between Dr. Pilkington and me was cemented forever.

I adored my high school journalism teacher, Bit Hunter, and loved being on the *LHS Review* staff. Therefore, I declared journalism to be my major. I also joined the staff of *The Daily Mississippian*. I wrote a story about homecoming and received a by-line that appeared on the front page. In my mind, I was ready for the *New York Times*, but I also knew deep inside that history and English were the subjects of interest to me.

Another professor I enjoyed was Dr. Kitchens in biology. He taught a required course often with over 300 students in Fulton Chapel. I found biology difficult and the class size overwhelming, but I thought Dr. Kitchens was an incredible lecturer.

Political science professor, Dr. Huey Howerton, was a favorite of many students, including William Winter. I wanted to take one of his classes but was discouraged by my advisor from doing so because not many girls took political science classes during the mid-1950s at Ole Miss. I made an appointment with Dr. Howerton to ask if he would object to my taking his introductory course during the first semester of my sophomore year. In his gentlemanly way, he assured me that I would be welcomed. The class was one of my favorites. Final exams in those days were held after the holidays. Grades were not posted until late January.

On January 30, 1957, Dr. Howerton sent me a postcard in Louisville on which he wrote: "You are not at all curious but you made an A; the only one in the class! Why can't I have more good students like you."

The history department had a number of fine professors in the 1950s. Among them were Drs. Margaret and John Moore. Both were outstanding teachers in their fields – Margaret in English history and John in Southern history. Margaret began each class by writing an outline of each day's lecture on the blackboard. She followed the outline, which was helpful to the students and helped us stay focused during her lectures. John came from a family of planters in Leland, Mississippi, in the heart of the Mississippi Delta, and understood the Deep South and its struggles with cotton production, race relations, and the Mississippi River in a way few did. He was always prepared and introduced me to writers and books on Southern history that have stayed with me through the years, such as John Hope Franklin's *From Slavery to Freedom*, A. D. Kirwin's *The Revolt of the Rednecks*, and W. J. Cash's *The Mind of the South*.

Dr. Jim Silver had a profound influence on many students, including me. He taught history classes with an emphasis on organized labor and race relations. Until Dr. Silver, I knew little about the labor movement and did not think as much as I should have about race. Many Mississippians did not like Dr. Silver and found his views too liberal. Efforts were made to drive him out of the university. I found his classes provocative. They were held in a small seminar room on the second floor of the library. No student skipped his classes because they were challenging and interesting.

Tom Hines was a year ahead of me in school. He was from Oxford and was a history major. He had a basement room in his parents' home on College Hill Road, where history students frequently gathered and had discussions of history and current events. Many of us were members of the Claiborne Society, an honorary club for history majors.

E. Grady Jolly and I entered Ole Miss as freshmen and took most of our classes together. We had fried donuts and a Coke at the alumni house grill many mornings for breakfast, walked the Grove talking about life, philosophy, politics, and the beginnings of our questioning about why white children and black children went to separate schools, played football games on Friday nights, but never against each other. We developed into thinking adults together at Ole Miss.

We attended each other's social functions and shared many good times together, but we had our moments too. For example, E. Grady was to take me to the "Back to School Street Dance" the night before classes were to begin in the fall semester of 1958, our senior year. The Street Dance was the biggest event of the year for those of us who had been at Ole Miss for several years. The streets around the Square were closed, and a popular band was brought in for the occasion. It was when we saw old friends we had been separated from over the summer and got the year rolling. It was my favorite event of the year, and E. Grady knew it.

About 5:00 p.m. on the afternoon of the Street Dance, E. Grady called to tell me he wanted to take Kay Haley from Columbus to the dance and he was sending someone in his stead to take me. He assured me that the person he was sending, Walker Watters, would be delightful company for me and that I would enjoy the evening. Walker had just graduated from Harvard and was coming to Ole Miss to law school. I was furious with E. Grady. Walker would not know anyone, would probably think the Street Dance was silly, and would ruin my evening.

I had no choice but to go along and so I dressed for the evening without any of the excitement all the other girls in the Chi Omega house were exhibiting. Then, there was a stillness in the house as one of the girls, who was in the downstairs living room, opened the front door to meet Walker, who said he was there to escort me to the dance. A buzz began to circulate around the house. I walked down the stairs to meet the most gorgeous, movie-star handsome person I had ever seen – Walker Watters from Jackson, Mississippi. We had a terrific time that evening. At every opportunity I could find, I waltzed by E. Grady with handsome Walker to make sure that he knew I was fine with his abandoning me for the evening. He had gotten my senior year off to a great start.

Jimmy Walker, a young man I had met at a political rally in Louisville in high school, was a tall, handsome, outgoing, friendly, energetic person who never met a stranger. He was destined for politics. We reconnected at Ole Miss. It was a symbiotic union of two people for whom the bonds of friendship would forever exist.

Jimmy, E. Grady, and I became a close-knit trio sharing many fun and loving times together.

One night, I had a date with Jimmy Melvin from Jackson for the KA formal. I had returned to school from a weekend with my parents in Louisville without my dress for the dance. I did not have a car and had no means of getting my dress in time for the formal. My mother said that she could put the dress on the bus from Louisville, but the bus did not come to Oxford. It did, however, stop in Pontotoc, but I did not have a car.

Jimmy had a car. He and E. Grady offered to take me to Pontotoc to retrieve my dress at the bus station if I would agree to treat them to dinner at the Embers in Memphis.

I accepted the offer because I was desperate. Jimmy was a first-year law student and wanted to show off his legal prowess. He drew up a formal contract on the back of a flyer announcing ticket sales for the 1957 Ole Miss-State game that said:

In consideration of the offer on the part of my friends, Grady Jolly and Jimmy Walker, to take me to Pontotoc, Miss. on Nov. 22, 1957, I, Mary Ann Strong, do hereby in consideration of the aforementioned offer, promise to take the above mentioned parties to wit: James Walker and Grady Jolly, to supper at the Embers Restaurant in Memphis, Tenn., on or before Dec. 20, 1957. I further promise that said meal may consist of any amount of food up to $20, as money is of no consequence when it comes to such loyal and true friends as these.

Signed this the 22nd day of Nov. 1957;

Mary Ann Strong

Witnesses:

Jimmy Walker

E. Grady Jolly, Jr.

Helen Rhyne

> The above mentioned maximum amount agreed to be spent on food for my friends is hereby agreed to be changed to $15.
>
> Signed: Mary Ann Strong

After the contractual obligation was fulfilled, it was noted on the document: Paid in Full this the 19th day of December 1957. James P. Walker.

Jimmy came to Louisville for visits, and I visited his home in Lambert. On the occasion of my first visit there, he had a sign made welcoming me to Lambert, "Home of Harry the Po Man's Friend." Jimmy's parents, Dr. and Mrs. Walker, were warm and welcoming to me.

Jimmy was dating Mary Ann Mobley during our first and second years at Ole Miss. When Sarah Longino from Jonestown, Mississippi, arrived at Ole Miss at the beginning of our junior year, Jimmy fell for her, and that was it for Mary Ann.

M y frenetic pace continued through my years at Ole Miss.

My freshman year at the university, I was elected president of my Chi Omega pledge class, president of Jr. Panhellenic, and president of the freshman YWCA. I was a member of the Committee of 100 that oversaw re-

The contract

ligious life on campus, a member of the Wesley Foundation, and piano accompanist for the university chorus.

I was a good student, but it was the potpourri of opportunities that enticed me, that kept me from facing the guilt that haunted me. When I was serving others, volunteering, I felt fulfilled. And I made many close friends during the process.

I also took my studies seriously, and when I served as scholarship chair for Chi Omega, I did my best to instill this value in the younger members.

I had a "Little Sister" in the group who did not share my view of the importance of scholarship. I felt it my responsibility to counsel her on the foolishness of her ways. I invited her upstairs to my room at the top of the stairs and spent an hour talking with her about the importance of studying and making good grades both for herself and for the scholastic reputation of Chi Omega on the campus.

The young woman shed tears and promised me that she would do much better. I believed her and felt good about fulfilling my responsibilities as scholarship chair.

A few minutes later, I heard gales of laughter coming up the stairs from the entrance hall directly under my room.

A group of her friends were joining her in the hilarity over my lecturing her and believing that she was sincere in her promises to me that she was going to do better.

During my sophomore year, I was elected secretary of the Associated Student Body in a campus-wide election. In my junior and senior years, I served as vice president and then president of Chi Omega and president of Mortar Board.

Although not a music major, I continued my love for music through accompanying the university chorus and taking organ for four years. I loved accompanying the chorus, but I was not really good enough to be doing that. I got through all the fall rehearsals, practices, and basic accompanying in a suitable manner, but when it came time to accompany the full chorus in performing "The Messiah," I knew that I could not do that. Thankfully, our choral music director agreed with me and asked Ms. Esther Oelrich to step in and accompany the group for the formal concert.

For four years I took organ from Ms. Oelrich in Fulton Chapel. I was never very good and did not practice enough to overcome my lack of natural talent. I learned to play "Jesu, Joy of Man's Desiring" and a Bach "Adagio" fairly well. Ms. Oelrich was always complimentary of me, but I think that was because she knew I loved music and wanted to do better than I had the natural talent to do.

Speaking of natural talent, intramural competitions on campus were big. The Chi Omegas played other sororities in sporting events and competed in decorating for homecoming. All the pledges had to participate in competitions whether we had any athletic ability or not. I had little to none.

I had to play in a basketball game against the Tri Deltas. Shirley Wagner (Crawford), an athletic Tri Delta, guarded me fiercely all through the game.

I never made a shot and got so frustrated when Shirley had me cornered once, I said, "Shirley, please let me just get rid of this ball! If you will let me out of this game, I'll never play basketball again for the rest of my life!"

Shirley showed me no mercy.

The Tri Deltas defeated us soundly, and no one in my sorority ever asked me to participate in a sporting event again.

However, I did have one athletic triumph during my years at Ole Miss. All students were required to take four semesters of physical education. One semester I enrolled in bowling.

We met twice a week at Kiamie's bowling alley, and we were assigned a partner for the semester. There were no mechanical pin-setters in those days, so one partner physically lined up the pins, then sat above them on a perch, while the other partner tossed the bowling ball.

During that time period, Jake Gibbs was Ole Miss's All American quarterback on the football team and All American catcher on the baseball team.

Jake was also my partner in bowling.

I had no athletic ability; Jake had enormous ability.

However, when grades were posted, I ended up with a "B".

Jake received a "C".

That would always be my one athletic claim to fame.

In 1955, Mary Ann Mobley and I attended a Sunday school class at Oxford-University Methodist Church. Dean Malcolm Guess, Dean of Students at Ole Miss, taught the class.

We were loyal attendees, and Mary Ann and I became even better friends. We took the class seriously and dutifully studied our lessons each week. We came prepared each Sunday and even took our lessons to one another's homes to study on weekends. We adored Dean Guess and wanted to do everything we could to please him not only because we loved him, but also because we were enriched by his lessons.

At the end of our freshman year, Dean Guess called us into his office in the "Y" Building.

"Mary Ann, Mary Ann," Dean Guess said, "I regret to tell you that you've both failed Wesley Hall Sunday School 101."

Mary Ann and I were stunned.

"You'll both need to retake the class next year."

We were humiliated and speechless.

Dean Guess continued, "You will need to come back to school in the fall a little early to meet with me to prepare —"Then a smile spread across Dean Guess' face, " …for the new entering freshman class — and you will work with me all year long."

Our punishment for "failing" was to help Dean Guess with the large group of the entering freshmen class of 1956. Mary Ann and I were thrilled — and relieved.

When September of 1956 arrived, Mary Ann and I felt like mature tutors of the freshmen class. Our first responsibility was to welcome the new students and pass around donuts and hot chocolate to make everyone feel welcomed. We sized up the freshmen and decided to divide the room. I offered to take the right side. There was a method in my madness. On the far right side of the room sat the most attractive boy I had ever seen — Dan Jordan.

My plan was to pass the donuts discretely to be sure that Dan could pick his favorite, and I might gain his favor.

After serving eight of the new students, I could see that the supply was dwindling. The most popular chocolate-filled ones were gone, but there were four glazed ones left.

Glancing ahead I noticed two students between Dan and me — two new boys from South Mississippi. I did not anticipate them being a problem. Surely, I thought, they would take only one each. That would leave Dan with two.

To my horror, the two new boys reached their huge hands over the platter and grabbed two donuts each. The tray was empty. There was nothing for me to offer Dan.

Of course, I was gracious about it, but I was furious with these two who had cost me the opportunity to incur the favor of Dan Jordan.

I'm generally the forgiving type, but just in case I encountered these boys in the future, I made a mental note of their names: Warner Alford and Robert Khayat.

10

At the beginning of my senior year at Ole Miss, the Air Force ROTC was attempting to recruit girls into the program by offering free flying lessons.

I was rooming with Ann Morris and Edwynne Joiner from Clarksdale, Mississippi. at the time. Ann was engaged to Ed Connell from Clarksdale, a certified flying instructor, who would be providing the flight instruction for the ROTC. He urged Ann to persuade some of her Chi Omega sisters, and especially her roommates, to sign up for the flight instruction.

Ann, Edwynne, and I all signed up to participate in the program. I do not recall whether either Ann or Edwynne went any further than to sign up, but I did. I began to take lessons from Ed. We had a series of on-the-ground lessons in the basics of aerodynamics, the parts of an aircraft, rules of flying, radio operation, and then we began actual instruction in the aircraft.

We flew a Cessna 150. It was outfitted with controls in both the pilot and co-pilot's positions. Ed took me out onto the tarmac at Clegg Field and taught me how to conduct a visual safety inspection of the aircraft before boarding. We looked under the wings for cracks, checked the tires for proper inflation, tested the fuel for condensation and level, and checked the engine oil. We then boarded the aircraft and ran through the checklist for mechanical inspection to prepare for takeoff.

When Ed was satisfied that all was in order, he instructed me to fasten my seat belt, secure any loose items in the cabin, and prepare for takeoff. He would then taxi the plane to the end of the runway, stop and rev up the engine to capacity with the brakes on for the last check. After being assured that all was in order, he would release the brakes and push the throttle forward. The plane needed to obtain 50 knots or 58 miles per hour before he would begin to pull back on the yoke for the plane to lift off.

After we reached a few hundred feet, Ed banked the plane to the left and continued climbing. When we reached an altitude of 2,000 feet, he would level off and being instructing me on how to do what he had just done.

Then we progressed to turns and traversed right and left above the campus until we moved into learning the stall technique. This meant that he raised the nose of the plane higher and higher until the wings lost all lift. We would then begin to fall. At exactly the right moment, Ed would pull back on the wheel, level the plane off, and then start this procedure all over again.

I did not like it and was always afraid during stall practice. It seemed to me that Ed always chose to go through this teaching process in the air above the football field because he loved to watch the team practicing below.

After I completed eight hours of flying time and successfully passed the written flight examination, Ed announced that it was time for me to solo. I was nervous but excited too. Ed walked out onto the runway with me, went through the visual inspection, and then told me to get in and take it from there. I was comfortable going through the checklist. The radio was on and I taxied down the runway for take off.

Ed told me to take a lap around Oxford and begin my landing approach to the field. He would be standing on the runway.

"If you are coming in appropriately for landing, I will not raise my arms into the air but will be holding onto my crutches," he said. "If I think you are not in line for a proper landing, I will raise my arms and wave you to take another trip around and begin your landing approach again."

That all sounded reasonable to me.

Ed had polio when he was about 11 and lost the use of his legs without crutches.

I taxied down to the east end of the runway, ran through the last checks, released the brakes, and pushed down on the throttle. Down the runway I flew until I thought I had reached the point for lift-off. I pulled back on the yoke and lifted off. All went fine. I banked left and felt a thrill of excitement that I could not imagine.

It was beautiful in the air on a crisp October day and all was going well until unexpectedly, it started to rain, not storming, but raining hard enough that I could not see out the front windows.

I did not know how to turn on the windshield wipers. In fact, I didn't know if airplanes had them.

I could not see except to look out of the window to my left at the land-marks below. I spotted Avent Acres, and knew it was time to begin to turn left, and return to the airport. I was beginning to panic.

Finally as I turned to face the runway, I could barely see to begin my descent.

I thought I saw Ed lifting his arms up as if to wave me on for another attempt, then he put them down, holding onto his crutches, signaling me to land.

I did not know what to do.

Panic was setting in. I decided I had to get out of that plane and get back on the ground one way or the other. I began the stalling procedure Ed had taught me and finally made a far less than perfect landing.

The plane stopped at the very last foot of runway.

When I taxied back to where Ed was stationed, he was upset.

"Get out. Get out!" he yelled.

I opened the cockpit door.

"You have no affinity for flying. Don't ever fly again," he demanded. Then Ed added, "You should get out of the ROTC program now."

11

While at Ole Miss, I had eight roommates. Mary Ann Doty from Tupelo and I roomed together our freshman year and the first semester of our sophomore year. She invited me on one occasion during our first year to come home with her to hear a high school classmate sing and play his guitar. She said he used to bring his guitar to school and beg fellow classmates to come sit under the tree in the schoolyard and listen to him sing.

I needed to study so declined the invitation that weekend. His name was Elvis Presley.

During the second semester of my sophomore year, I roomed with Melinda Gwin from Indianola, Mississippi.

Mary Ann Mobley and I roomed together our junior year in the Chi Omega house.

Mary Ann was extremely popular on the campus. We had only one telephone in the sorority house. It rang all the time — and most of the calls were for Mary Ann Mobley.

One September afternoon, someone answered the phone and shouted down the hall, "Mary Ann, phone for you."

I ran to the phone.

I recognized the voice on the other end as an attractive boy on campus.

"Mary Ann," he said, "I am calling to invite you to be my date for the NROTC ball in April.

I thought it was odd that he was calling eight months in advance, but I was thrilled.

"I would love to go with you," I replied.

"You mean you are really free? How wonderful!" he said.

Then there was a long, dead silence, and he asked, "This is Mobley, isn't it?"

After Mary Ann Mobley won Miss America, she did not come back to school for our senior year, so I roomed with Edwynne Joiner and Ann

Miss Ole Miss and Phil Berry, Col. Rebel

Morris from Clarksdale, and then Suzy Butler from Jonestown and Mary Katie Gillis from McComb.

Through the years, I heard some female friends and classmates say that they were not interested in their education at Ole Miss, that they were there to have a "good time," to meet a husband, and develop the social skills necessary to expand their lives after college. Many did not prepare themselves to work outside the home and never expected to do so.

That was not the case for me. I went to Ole Miss to get an education and to decide what I wanted to do with my life. My undergraduate days at the University of Mississippi gave me a solid foundation in the liberal arts and involvement with people whose life experiences and viewpoints were different from mine. They also prepared me for a job I could have never envisioned at the time.

The highest honor bestowed upon me during my college years was being selected as one of six inductees to the University of Mississippi Hall of Fame. The Hall of Fame selection was made by *The Daily Mississippian* staff and a 25-member secret committee. Selection was based on leadership, scholarship, and service to the University.

On a freezing November afternoon in the fall of 1958, Phil Berry and I were crowned Colonel Rebel and Miss Ole Miss during halftime at the Ole Miss-Mississippi State football game. The excitement and pleasure of the moment eclipsed the freezing weather. Phil's parents and my parents were seated in the stadium as we entered the field to receive this honor in front of more than 40,000 Ole Miss fans. Naturally, the *Winston County Journal* wrote extensively about my selection, which seemed to please my parents immensely.

To be elected Colonel Rebel and Miss Ole Miss was to enjoy the support of our friends. In many ways, it was a popularity contest. There were honors far more prestigious than this one, and more deserving of attention, but for the moment to be recognized by our peers was a moment of great pride for us both.

Phil was an engineering major from Laurel, Mississippi. I was a history and English major from Louisville. Mississippi.

Phil was an accomplished tennis player and the first non-football student-athlete ever nominated or elected Colonel Rebel. He later became a renowned orthopedic surgeon in Dallas, Texas.

12

I met Bill Connell from Clarksdale, Mississippi, during the summer before my senior year at Ole Miss. My roommate, Ann Morris, from Clarksdale, was marrying Ed Connell, his first cousin. They arranged for Bill, an attractive 33-year-old bachelor, to take me to one of the wedding parties.

They had also arranged for me to have a date with Kenneth Williams the next night. When Kenneth came to pick me up, Bill drove up and said that he thought he would just go along with us.

That ended whatever courtship Kenneth and I might have had.

Bill and I dated during my senior year, and he proposed to me in his car outside Sarah Longino's house in Jonestown, Mississippi, shortly after Christmas of that year. Sarah's father had a practice of flashing the front porch lights on and off until Sarah and her house guests got out of the car with their dates and came into the house. He had the lights flashing while Bill was proposing, but we lingered long enough for me to say yes.

Bill gave me an engagement ring crafted by Bourgeois Jewelers in Jackson. They crafted the ring using a gorgeous diamond his grandmother had given him and two smaller baguettes on each side.

Celebration of our engagement began immediately with a party in the Mississippi Delta. The guests consisted mainly of Bill's Delta friends, but we also included a number of my Ole Miss friends. That was the first time I was truly aware of the 11-year age difference.

A few weeks after the party, Bill asked me to go to Memphis with him to a Cotton Carnival party. I told him I couldn't go because the party was in the middle of exam week. He was furious.

Perhaps that should have been a sign of things to come, but I didn't think much of it at the moment.

I graduated from Ole Miss on May 31, 1959. Bill was there and joined in the celebration, which was both a joy and a sorrow for me. A part of my life I loved was ending.

Shortly after graduation from Ole Miss in late May 1959, my mother and I went to Jackson to look for a wedding dress. The wedding was scheduled for September.

I tried on several dresses until we found the perfect one — just what I wanted. But, as I stood in the dress and looked at myself in the mirror, my eyes filled with tears.

I was not ready to get married and make the commitment marriage required. I was not ready to give up my dreams. Dreams of living in other parts of the country. Dreams of working before settling down into domestic life.

We did not buy the dress. We simply returned to Louisville.

The next day I went to Clarksdale to meet with Bill.

I drove to Bill's home at Rena Lara, a small community southwest of Clarksdale adjacent to the Mississippi River. We sat on the swing on the front porch. The sun was setting over the levee that held the Mississippi River from the fields of cotton planted up to its edge. As we sat on the porch, the Four Freshman song, "I remember April," played on the radio.

"Bill," I said, as the porch swing moved slowly back and forth, "I'm not ready to be married." Bill looked shocked.

"I love you," I said, "but I want to experience more of life before I marry and settle in the Delta."

I took off his beautiful engagement ring and handed it back to him.

I could see the pain in his eyes. He loved me and he was ready finally to marry. I knew he was humiliated and embarrassed. He was going to have to face his friends and family and tell them that the woman he had announced he was going to marry had backed out of the wedding.

I drove back to Louisville alone.

I had left the magical world of Ole Miss and had lost my moorings. I was separated from my friends, and I had just ended an engagement.

I knew I wasn't ready for marriage, but I did not know where to go or what to do.

13

After I ended the engagement with Bill, I decided to move to New York. I'd always dreamed of living in Manhattan. I found a job conducting research for Chase Manhattan Bank, providing information on South American countries in which the bank was considering making loans.

My salary would be $550 a month.

I told the human resources person at the bank I could not live on that in New York. "Then," he said, "you should go west and reach out for adventure there."

I met an attractive young man in the city who had recently graduated from Yale. He extolled the virtues of the university and convinced me I needed to go to Yale and enroll in a graduate program in French.

I had taken only 18 hours of French in undergraduate school, but it sounded like a good idea.

I was running low on money, so had no choice but to call my father and tell him about this exciting new adventure. I was certain he would understand that I needed him to finance this next step.

When I asked my father for the money, there was dead silence.

"Mary Ann," he eventually said, "I am sending you a ticket home. How much money do you have left?"

I told him I had enough to pay for a taxi to the airport and get a cup of coffee and donut for breakfast.

"Then call the taxi, get the donut, and pick up your ticket that I will have wired to you at the airport. You have had enough of your New York experience."

The next morning, I was on the plane back to Mississippi.

I decided to follow the advice of the Chase Manhattan human resources person. I went west — to Glendora, California, in July of 1959.

I spent several weeks with my close friend from Louisville, Freemie, and her husband, Bob Stone.

Freemie was three years older than me.

Bob was from Roanoke, Virginia, and a graduate of the University of Virginia. I adored Bob. He was smart, attractive, well read, and an engaging conversationalist on almost any subject. He was also exceptionally kind. Bob was an engineer with Aerojet General in the space program.

Glendora was a beautiful town in the foothills of the San Bernardino mountains, approximately thirty miles east of Pasadena. Freemie and Bob toured me around the greater Los Angeles area and introduced me to a world I had not seen before.

I fell in love with the area and applied for a teaching job at the Glendora Junior High School, where Freemie taught seventh-grade English and social studies.

However, there was a problem: I did not have a teacher's license and was not qualified to teach in the California public school system.

The principal suggested that if I could obtain some letters of recommendation, he might be able to have me approved on a probationary basis to teach. I called on Dean Malcolm Guess at Ole Miss. I did not see the letter he wrote on my behalf, but it must have been glowing. Soon after its arrival I was offered a job teaching eighth-grade English and social studies at Glendora Junior High School at a salary of $550 per month.

I loved the children in my classes; however, I did not love the teaching materials I was provided, or the casual approach to grammar the California school system put forward.

I sent back to Mississippi for the strict grammar and social studies materials used in our schools and adapted them as best I could to the requirements of California.

Dean Guess, Mary Ann, and Bill, graduation day 1959

The semester in school went well. The students and their parents seemed to like me. Frequently on Thursday evenings, the school sponsored dances for the junior high school students and asked the teachers to chaperone the occasions. We were paid $5.00 for each event. One day a young male teacher and I were standing in the hall as our students filed into class. He asked if I was going to chaperone the dance that evening. I replied that I was because I enjoyed the dances — and because I needed the $5.00 pay.

"Why in the world do you need the extra money?" he asked.

"Because I am buying a car and need all the help I can get in making my monthly payments," I said.

"What are you being paid to teach?" he asked.

"$550 a month," I responded. "What are you being paid?"

"$750 a month," he said.

I suggested to him that it did not seem fair that he would be paid so much more than me when we both had B.A. degrees in history and English, were both without a teacher's license, and neither had any teaching experience.

"Do you think that seems right?" I asked.

"Of course," he said, "because I am a man, and I have responsibilities."

I wondered what those responsibilities might be since he was single too. We were performing the same work, with the same educational background, in the same work environment.

I didn't comment because I was a product of the times — a time when women did not openly disagree with men.

I found a room to rent in a nice home near the school. However, all was not as it appeared. There was a son living in the home a little older than me, who made me uncomfortable. The family shouted at each other, played the radio loud, and lived a different lifestyle from the one to which I was accustomed.

My mother had arranged for me to go by for a visit in the home of a couple, Mr. and Mrs. Charles Mathews, who lived up on one of the mountains overlooking Glendora. Mr. Mathews had been in the Army in World War II with my mother's friend from Louisville, Syd Jordan. While there, I told them that I was having a difficult time adjusting to my living situation in Glendora. They said they would like to invite their neighbor across the street to come over and meet me.

Their neighbor, Mrs. Harold, lived in an English stone house overlooking Glendora with a view of both the mountains and the valley. She was recently widowed and lonely. She asked if I would like to rent a room in her home. I was thrilled because she was nice, refined, and everything I could have wanted.

Mrs. Harold and I got along well and frequently had dinner together in the evenings. We watched the Miss America pageant together. She was as excited as was I when my sorority sister Lynda Mead was crowned Miss America in the fall of 1959.

14

Mrs. Harold introduced me to her bridge friends and to a couple who were members of Grace Episcopal Church in Glendora, Dr. and Mrs. Baxter. The Baxters invited me to come visit Grace Church the following Sunday, which I did and loved it. I began confirmation classes and was confirmed into the Episcopal Church at Grace Church in Glendora in January of 1960.

I soon met a young man who had a leadership role in the church. We began to attend concerts and the Pasadena Playhouse together. He took me to the Hollywood Bowl and to a UCLA-USC game in the coliseum. We were attending a performance in the Pasadena Playhouse the night of the 1959 Ole Miss-LSU football game. Even though he had no interest in Ole Miss football, he found the game for me on the radio as we rode to Pasadena, and I was elated that Ole Miss was winning. When we left the Playhouse and turned the radio on again, I heard the infamous Billy Cannon run and had tears in my eyes, which left him mystified as to how anyone, especially a young woman, could care so much about a football game. He had no idea how heartbroken I was for all the members of the Ole Miss team who had been my schoolmates at Ole Miss.

I made many friends in Glendora, dated a number of young men, and was beginning to put down roots in the community. As the weeks and months moved on, however, I realized how much I missed Bill.

I had made a mistake in breaking off our engagement.

I wrote Bill a letter and told him how much I regretted my actions — along with a long explanation of all the thoughts, dreams, and impulsiveness that led me to the decision.

I did not expect to hear back from him. I knew he was hurt, embarrassed, mortified by what I had done.

About a week later, Mrs. Harold retrieved the mail and handed me a letter postmarked Rena Lara, Mississippi.

She quickly disappeared, discerning, I think, that I needed to read this letter in privacy.

As I opened the letter, I couldn't imagine how he would respond to my rambling explanations and apologies.

The letter was one sentence long.

"What color do you want to paint the bedroom?"

IV
The Delta

15

Bill called and said he was coming to California to visit at Thanksgiving. He wanted to see if we could pick up our relationship.

Bill said because of the hurt and embarrassment over the break-up and cancellation of the wedding, he would not go through a big wedding in the Mississippi tradition as we had originally planned.

If we were going to be married, he insisted, it would be a quiet event in California with no family or friends.

I knew the heartbreak this would cause my parents, and his, but I agreed.

We set the date for February 3, 1960.

I told my school principal of my desire to be released from my contract. He reluctantly agreed and wished me well.

Bill and I were married at 11:00 a.m. on Wednesday, February 3, 1960, in the chapel of Grace Episcopal Church in Glendora, California. Eight people attended.

I wore a champagne-colored Christian Dior suit I had bought at Bullock's in Pasadena. I carried a prayer book topped with a white orchid. The ceremony was short and meaningful. I was sorry that my parents and Bill's parents were not there, but I knew they were there in spirit supporting us.

After the ceremony, Freemie and Bob hosted a brunch for us. The day was beautiful, as are most Southern California days. We were surrounded by a small but loving group of friends and supporters. We left mid-afternoon in my Nash Rambler and drove to the Ojai Valley Inn near Ventura, California. We then drove up the Coastal Highway to San Francisco, where we stayed at the St. Francis Hotel.

Wedding day

After San Francisco, we drove through the central part of the state and saw all the vast farming that took place in some of the areas. Eventually we arrived in Las Vegas, where we met Elsie and Bill Heaton at the Sands. Sammie Davis, Jr., Frank Sinatra, Dean Martin, Peter Lawford, and Joey Bishop -- the famous "Rat Pack" -- sat at a table next to us.

As we drove to Mississippi from Las Vegas, Bill said, "We aren't going to get a dog."

I looked over at him. I had never mentioned a dog.

"Every newly married couple gets a dog and carries on like fools. We are not going to do that so don't ever bring a stray dog onto the place."

On the drive, we also had our first marital fight. We were discussing the American involvement in the Korean War. Bill waxed on and on about what a mistake our country had made by not invading farther north in Korea. I spoke just as forcefully about how wrong I thought that would have been. That was the first time I realized how far apart he and I were in our political thinking.

Bill served in both World War II and the Korean War. His military service influenced his thinking along more nationalistic lines than my more global approach to political issues. I had developed my own opinions during my college years on racial integration, voting rights for minorities, the ending of apartheid in South Africa, equal opportunities for women, and similar issues that were at the forefront of discussion by many college students.

Bill was a son of the Mississippi Delta, where views on race and social justice concerns were far more conservative than mine. By the time we were married, Bill had been farming for over ten years. He was surrounded, for the most part, by people who shared his positions on these issues.

And that most Southern of places was about to be my home.

16

After Bill and I married in California, we returned to Clarksdale, Mississippi, and settled into married life on the Connell Plantation in Rena Lara, Mississippi, where Bill had lived for eight years. We lived in a white frame, two-bedroom, one-bath, house. It — and the plantation— were owned by my new father-in-law, but Bill farmed the land.

I looked forward to married life, and I was excited about setting up housekeeping. But my excitement was brought to a halt the morning after we arrived. Laura, who had been Bill's house-keeper for eight years, came into the bedroom as I was placing my clothes in one of the two closets.

"Mr. Billy is not going to like this," she said. "You moved his good clothes and his work clothes into one closet."

I took the other closet for my clothes. Laura continued to chastise me.

"Mr. Billy doesn't ever put his good clothes and work clothes in the same closet."

I did not respond and continued to unpack and divide the space for us. It seemed equitable in my mind.

Laura lived in a small house behind our house and came to work for us every day. She adored "Mr. Billy."

A few weeks after I moved in, Bill came home from the one-room Rena Lara post office with a puppy.

I remembered our conversation in the car on the drive back from California. And I knew then that Bill had a much softer spot in his heart than he let most people see.

We named the puppy "Post Office." She endeared herself to both of us and also to Laura. Post Office would walk to meet Laura every morning when she came to work and stay with her all day. When Laura left to go to her home in the afternoon, Post Office would walk her home.

Post Office gave birth to a litter of seven puppies. Shortly thereafter, she died while being spayed. I will never forget when we received the call from Dr. Gates' office telling us that Post Office had "expired" during the surgery. I wasn't sure what the term meant and could not believe that we would not be bringing her home the next morning. I was heartbroken, as were Laura and Bill.

Post Office had been the one piece of the Delta that was mine. I loved her — and she returned unconditional love — when I was still trying to adapt to my new environment. We decided to keep the last of her litter of seven and named him "Seven." He became our new pet and our joy. After that Bill always welcomed pets into our family's life.

Laura and I bonded over Post Office. And, eventually, we found a mutual respect for each other. We even shared a degree of affection, but she never got used to a woman living with "Mr. Billy" and intruding on her terrain.

Moving to the Mississippi Delta was a strange experience for me. I had no idea a state as small as Mississippi could house two strikingly different worlds – the "Delta" and the "Hills." The way of life, the view of life, the value systems, and the way money was handled could not have been further apart. Adjusting to the Delta culture was difficult for me, compounded by the fact that Bill was eleven years older than me.

"My country is the Mississippi Delta, the river country," wrote William Alexander Percy in his classic, *Lanterns on the Levee*. "It lies flat, like a badly drawn half oval, with Memphis at its northern and Vicksburg at its southern tip." Another Greenville native, David Cohn, described the region when he wrote, "The Mississippi Delta begins in the lobby of the Peabody Hotel in Memphis and ends on Catfish Row in Vicksburg." The Delta is a 250-mile stretch of land that lies between Highway 61, also known as the Blues Highway, and the Mississippi River. It is bordered on the west by the Mississippi River and on the east by a ridge of hills just beyond the

Yazoo River. This alluvial plain, formed by centuries of the Mississippi River over-flowing its banks and depositing annual layers of silt on what was once a vast depression between the river and the hills, is what we call "the Delta." North and south it measures 196 miles, east and west at the widest point fifty miles.

Initially this was a land of unbroken forests, where all trees grew there except pine and, strangely enough, the magnolia, Mississippi's state tree and flower. When slavery became unprofitable in the older Southern states and slave-holders began to look for cheap fertile lands farther west, younger sons from Virginia, South Carolina, and Kentucky started a migration into the Delta. They cleared the forests, settled on the banks and bends of the Mississippi River, and eventually formed towns, such as Friars Point, Greenville, and Vicksburg, Mississippi.

In the rich soil of the alluvial plain, cotton grew in abundance. Slaves and sharecroppers alike grew and picked the cotton, and Memphis businessmen began to market and sell it. Cotton became king, and Memphis became the Delta's unofficial capital. For years, the Mississippi River was the main thoroughfare, transporting not only cotton to New Orleans, St. Louis, and Chicago, but bringing to the region ethnic influences from all over. Italian, Lebanese, Jewish and Chinese communities sprang up and down the riverside and brought a unique culture to the area.

Wealth and poverty lived side by side in the Delta. Vast fortunes were made from growing cotton. At one time, the counties in the Mississippi Delta were some of the wealthiest areas in the world.

When I arrived in the Delta in 1960, the glory days of cotton and wealth were nearing their end. The price of farm equipment was skyrocketing, and foreign competition was driving down the price of Delta cotton. By my "Hill" standards, wealth still existed far greater than I had ever seen. And Deltans spent money as if there were an endless supply. A few spent it even if they didn't have it. They didn't give a second thought to going to the bank to borrow money to maintain their lifestyle.

The Connells were deeply involved with the world of cotton. My father-in-law, Bill, Sr., and his twin brother, Willis Connell, started their cotton merchant business, Connell Brothers, in 1931, when they were 26 years old. They never had private offices and worked across a large planter's desk from each other for 50 years. They never had a cross word and had an agreement that if they both did not agree on a transaction, then they would not enter into it. They were successful and respected. Calvin Turley at the Memphis Cotton Museum once told me that Bill and Willis were so highly respected in the industry that when they introduced him to people in the cotton business, he had instant credibility because of their reputation of integrity in the business.

My first few years in the Delta felt like an endless party. There was the annual Planter's Ball in Clarksdale, the annual Phi Delta Theta party, the Cotton Carnival parties in Memphis, the parties given every time anyone had guests visit from out of town, dinner parties, and huge cocktail parties.

The parties were extravagant. Some I will never forget.

The events surrounding the wedding of Katherine Anderson were lavish. The Andersons were large landowners and had entertained extensively through the years for others. When their daughter, Katherine, became engaged, the north Delta turned out in high numbers to entertain.

My friend Greenie Carr McKee, who married John McKee in December of 1959 before Bill and I married in February 1960, and I hosted a luncheon for Katherine in our home at Rena Lara. We decided to serve scotch sours made in a blender with a can of frozen lemonade and a can of scotch. None of us drank much then and had no idea that a sweet, fruity drink could have the effect it did. Consequently, we talked and drank scotch sours until nearly 2:00 p.m. before we served lunch.

Greenie and I went to Memphis in anticipation of our party and bought pistachio ice cream and raspberry sherbet to make a watermelon mold to have brought into the dining room on a silver tray to display and slice to the raves of our guests. While Earnestine, my helper, was unmolding the dessert in my un-air conditioned kitchen and placing the frozen watermelon mold

Laura Whitehead, Mary Ann, and Post Office

on the silver tray, it melted. When Earnestine walked into the dining room and placed the tray in front of Greenie to carve and serve, Greenie looked down and saw nothing but a puddle of brown melted ice-cream and sherbet on the tray. Instead of praises, our guests responded, "Oh, well, let's just have another scotch sour!"

All of the young people enjoyed the parties at the Andersons because they were quite glamorous, more like the Great Gatsby than Mississippi. The Andersons traveled all over the world. Gertrude Anderson often brought back rare perfumes from their travels. Along with Katherine, many others of us would secretly gather in Gertrude's large bathroom and sneak a touch of her perfume.

Bill had friends of all ages and had entertained for years at his home at Rena Lara before we married. We continued his traditions together and hosted events both large and small. My first dinner party as a young wife was a disaster. Bill was an excellent cook and had hosted many a dinner party, yet I wanted to prepare and do everything myself for my first dinner party.

Our guests were Elsie and Bill Heaton, who had been at our wedding in California, and Syd and Allen Sessions, two of Bill's oldest and closest friends. I found a recipe for shrimp pilaf, purchased all the ingredients, lined them up on the counter when the guests arrived, but I had prepared nothing. I thought it would take only a few minutes to put the meal together. It took two hours. By the time I finally served dinner, it was 10:00 p.m., and our guests were exhausted — and they'd had too much drink.

In 1960 and 1961, we entertained many of my college friends, which was fun for me. Bill was marvelous at mixing them with his friends, who were older, and we all had a great time together. I was now enjoying many of his friends and beginning to feel at home with them. My friends and his friends began to mix frequently. We had dozens of dinner parties attended by a blend of our two groups.

Mary Eva and Curt Presley lived on the adjoining farm to ours at Rena Lara. Bill and Curt had been friends all of their lives. Curt was an intelligent man with a myriad of interests similar to Bill's. They were both "people" persons, who were somewhat misplaced as farmers. I loved to cook, and Curt loved to eat. I frequently made pies in the middle of the afternoons. I could count on Curt showing up just to check on us exactly at the time I pulled a chocolate pie out of the oven.

Each September, Oscar Connell, Bill's younger brother, hosted a dove hunt at the Baugh Plantation. Anne Connell, my sister-in-law, with help from Tankie, my mother-in-law, always served delicious food, and a large crowd attended. After the men hunted doves in the afternoon, we all joined together back at the lodge at the Baugh Plantation for drinks, dinner, and the perennial craps games.

After the meal was served, the dining room table was cleared and covered with a felt cloth to serve as a dice table. Huge sums of money were placed in the middle of the table as each player tossed the dice.

At my first dove hunt, Lee Pryor, a young woman from Calhoun City, was standing next to me. We watched the spectacle. Her husband was in his medical residency at one of the hospitals in Memphis. She and I were the same age.

As we stood watching the craps game, she leaned over and said, "There is more money lying on that table for this roll of the dice than my husband earns in a year."

The early 1960s were filled with weddings of my friends. Sarah Longino and Jimmy Walker were married at St. George's Episcopal Church in Clarksdale on September 30, 1960; Edwynne Joiner, one of my college roommates, and Robert Love were married at St. George's on May 19, 1962. Parties were thrown for both couples, capped with lovely receptions in Delta style at the Clarksdale Country Club.

Among the most popular of the Clarksdale parties were the Connell and Abraham International Quail Suppers hosted by Bill and his friend, A.C. Abraham, from 1951 to 1959, at the Connells' lodge at Sherard, outside of Clarksdale. Since the hosts capped the guest list at ten couples, invitations were cherished.

Bill's mother, Tankie, cooked the quail and trimmings for the gatherings, and the food was exceptional. Printed menus, written in Arabic, were distributed to the guests. Bill and A.C. required that each guest or guest couple perform a skit at the event. Bill and A.C. judged the skits and awarded a grand prize for the best skit of the evening.

I was invited to the International Quail Supper for the first time in 1959, when I was still a senior at Ole Miss. I had to perform a skit. I dressed as Minnie Pearl, played my ukulele, and sang "You Are My Sunshine."

I did not rise to the level of performance that was the standard for the Quail Supper, but at least I participated and got a passing grade for being a good sport.

Martha Jane Tomlinson and Billy Howell won the prize that evening for their costumes. Martha Jane had dyed long-handled underwear purple and made a spaceship from cardboard. She and Billy came as the "Purple People Eaters" and read a poem poking fun at each of the guests.

One of the most notable of the skits was when Bill's brother, Oscar, dressed as a farmer and sang "Old McConnell Had a Farm." Each time a verse was introduced, Oscar had one of the farm workers outside the door waiting to thrust the animal being sung about into the midst of the party. Soon the lodge at Sherard was filled with goats, pigs, etc.

After Oscar's skit, Tankie said, "No more Quail Supper parties at the lodge. You have gone too far. Go someplace else for all this nonsense!"

Bill and A.C. gave souvenir gifts each year, similar to the favors purchased from the Balfour Company and given as favors at fraternity parties at Ole Miss — a pitcher, mug, and cigar box. Because Martha Jane and Billy were not married at the time of the 8th International Quail Supper, they each received one of the pitchers, the souvenir favor of the evening.

My sister-in-law, Anne Connell, described these events as "creative and lots of fun." "Billy and A.C.," she said "went to the ends of the earth to make everyone have a good time, and we did."

17

Amidst all the fun and frivolity of my early married days, I found a quiet respite and safe haven in a beautiful room at 227 Clark Street in Clarksdale with a new friend, Claudia Money Luckett. Money was two days younger than I. Her birthday was October 14, 1937; mine was October 12, 1937.

Money and I became companions and confidants from the first day we met, bound together by our mutual interest in music and books. We spent hours together listening to opera, reading the librettos, and endlessly discussing who we thought sang which roles best. We did the same with books. Money loved literature of the Middle Ages, which I did not care for at all until she encouraged me to read one of her favorites, *Kristin Lavransdatter* by Sigrid Undset, which I loved. While I never became a devotee of medieval literature, Money broadened my literary interests and opened my mind and heart to many books I would never have read without her encouragement.

Money was the second of four children of Celeste "Kellye" and Semmes Luckett. Kellye was a tall, vibrant, entertaining woman with deep roots in the Clarksdale community. Semmes was a lawyer and a leader in the conservative movement in Mississippi, especially in matters of racial segregation. Their first child, Celeste Hill, became Miss Mississippi in 1954; next came Money, followed by Semmes, Jr.; and several years later, Lucretia. The Luckett family were devout members of St. Elizabeth's Catholic Church in Clarksdale.

In November 1949, when she was twelve, Money complained of headaches, fever, and aching limbs. "Scarlatina," said the doctor called in to treat Money. "Polio," whispered her mother. "Check her for polio," Kellye asked the doctor.

In 1948-49, poliomyelitis, or infantile paralysis, was on a rampage in this country. In 1948, the March of Dimes reported 27,726 cases nationally. In 1949, the number rose to 42,033. Of those, 359 were in Mississippi, and Money was one of them.

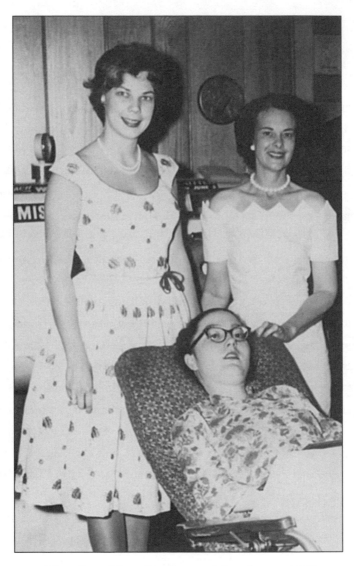

Mary Ann, Money Luckett, and friend, circa 1963

Prior to the attack of polio in November 1948, Money had lived an active life riding horses, swimming, and playing basketball. Polio robbed Money of these joys of her childhood and of the ability to ever breathe on her own again.

The polio virus attacked her central nervous system. Her spinal cord no longer sent messages to the muscles in her shoulders, arms, and legs. Breathing was hopeless because the muscles needed to bellow her lungs were inoperative.

She lived in an 800-pound metal chamber (the "Iron Lung") with a vacuum diaphragm which did the breathing for her.

Money was a quadriplegic. She could turn her head, move her eyes and blink. She could pick up food with a spoon or fork and feed herself. She could chew food and swallow. Other than that, her physical capacity was severely limited. She was dependent on others to bathe, clean, and dress her in her daily ritual of living.

Money did not leave her home for years because of her dependency on the Iron Lung that enabled her to live.

Money was an exceptional person. In spite of her physical limitations, her mind was alive and functioning on all cylinders always. She engaged in life-long learning experiences with a remarkable attitude and determination. She became president of the Friends of Carnegie Public Library in Clarksdale and was one of the Delta Arts Council organizers. She was named a Paul Harris Fellow for outstanding community service by the Clarksdale Rotary Club. She was awarded a college diploma from Nazareth College of Nazareth, Kentucky.

Money pursued not only reading, but also writing. She carried on a daily writing correspondence with notable people, including William F. Buckley, Jr.; Kevin Lynch, former articles editor of *National Review*; Linton Weeks, editor of *Southern Magazine* and later the *Washington Post*; and Sam Cohen, inventor of the neutron bomb. She was able to do this through the contribution of a typewriter given to her by IBM, which she used with three fingers of her left hand. From a surgical procedure by which a muscle was removed from the palm of her right hand and inserted into the thumb of her left hand, she was able to turn pages of a book. Highly regarded people traveled from all over the world to meet her. James Melton, the opera singer, visited her and sang for her in her room, as did Maria Newman (daughter of Alfred Newman) and Alberto Esposito.

My times with Money were, perhaps, my best moments in the Mississippi Delta.

My dear friend and mentor Dean Malcolm Guess died on September 19, 1961. Dean Guess was a legend in his own time at Ole Miss. He attended the University of Mississippi from 1908 to 1913. In 1923, the university hired him to serve as general secretary of the YMCA. In 1947, he became dean of men. He served Ole Miss until he retired from the university in 1955 as dean emeritus of students.

Dean Guess was a defining personality in my life, as he was in the lives of many other students. He was always available to talk to me. As I wrestled with new thoughts and ideas that had not been a part of my mindset, Dean Guess sat with me for hours on the front steps of the Oxford-University Methodist Church. He listened to me patiently as I told him about my rising doubts surrounding religion, God, Christianity, the Methodist Church, and racism.

Unwavering in his own faith, Dean Guess was a sounding board to a college student struggling to make sense out of so many thoughts, ideas, and doubts. He encouraged me to question, to doubt, to read, to think — and to never lose sight of the teachings of Jesus no matter where my questioning — from miracles to the virgin birth — might take me.

The funeral was held at the Oxford-University Methodist Church. Dozens of his former students made tributes to this great man, a man whose influence was life-shaping for me.

A few days after his funeral, the Mississippi Legislature passed a resolution honoring Dean Guess and lauding him "for making himself continuously available to students and faculty, for counseling and consultation on myriad problems with generous sympathy, concern, and love." One of the authors of the resolution was state Representative J.P. Coleman (also a former governor) of Choctaw County. Mr. Coleman's entrance to the university, in 1932, was made possible when Dean Guess accepted a load of potatoes in lieu of his matriculation fee.

18

Publicly, Bill and I lived a carefree Delta life, but privately we struggled. We desperately wanted to start a family. Between 1960 and 1962, I suffered four miscarriages.

After the fourth miscarriage, Dr. Marascalco delivered the news: *I was a habitual aborter.* He was skeptical that I would ever carry a child to term.

My best friend, Greenie McKee, knew of our difficulties, as did our parents and Laura, but publicly, we put on smiles and went about our life.

The Huntley-Brinkley Report was one of the most popular and widely-viewed television news programs from 1956-1970. In addition to the nightly news program, David Brinkley, a native of Wilmington, North Carolina, produced several feature stories each year on different parts of the country in a documentary series called "David Brinkley's Journal."

One of these stories was "Our Man on the Mississippi."

In 1963, Brinkley embarked on a feature story on "Ole Man River," the mighty Mississippi River from its inception in Lake Itasca in Northern Minnesota to its entry into the Gulf of Mexico. Along the way, he stopped at Rena Lara, Mississippi, our home, to film the exact spot at Sunflower Landing where Hernando DeSoto — on May 8, 1541 — discovered the Mississippi River. Bill and Curt Presley helped Brinkley and his three-man crew navigate the levee and the gumbo soil until they could get the shot of the river they wanted.

About 11:00 a.m. on the morning of the shooting at Sunflower Landing, Bill told me that he had invited Mr. Brinkley and his crew to have lunch at our home at Rena Lara.

*David Brinkley and Bill, during
Brinkley's visit to the Mississippi Delta*

I panicked. We had no groceries. I had nothing in our home to serve the crew.

We were 15 miles away from the nearest grocery store in Clarksdale. Bill calmly said, "No problem. I will take care of it."

Bill went across the road to the Chinaman's store at Rena Lara. He bought several packages of hot dogs, buns, a jar of mustard, and paper plates. He served David Brinkley and his crew hot dogs from our kitchen.

I learned much from Bill in situations such as this. He was always relaxed. He enjoyed entertaining, whether it be hot dogs in the kitchen or a formal dinner at one of the Delta's high moments. All that mattered to him was enjoying the company and having a good time.

Bill had loved photography since he was eight years old and received his first camera as a Christmas gift. He was rarely without it and took pictures of everything from workers picking cotton to parties and weddings. He took remarkable pictures of the fire that destroyed the Alcazar Hotel and much of downtown Clarksdale on March 16, 1947.

He eventually started a business photographing children and families in natural light, something that was seldom done anywhere in the country at that time. He opened an office in the Bobo Building on Sunflower Avenue in Clarksdale and expanded his photography efforts into taking pictures of weddings, which was profitable but also stressful.

19

Our first daughter was born on April 7, 1963. We named her Elizabeth Strong Connell in honor of my grandfather Strong's sister, Elizabeth Strong Huling. My grandfather called her "Sister;" I called her "Aunt Sister." She was tall, outgoing, strikingly beautiful, a great dancer, an excellent bridge player, and an interesting conversationalist. She was born at "Stronghold," a plantation on the banks of the Yazoo River, near Greenwood, Mississippi. After the death of her father, John Strong, her mother, my grandfather Strong, and Aunt Sister moved to New Orleans, where they lived on Esplanade Street along with four additional daughters born there.

Aunt Sister made her debut in the ballroom at the St. Charles Hotel in New Orleans. As she walked in, a young man working as a desk clerk was stricken by her beauty, her snow white hair, and her charm. He told a co-worker when he ended work that night, he was going to rent a full dress suit, go to the ball, and dance with her. His name was Harry Huling. He and Aunt Sister married and moved to Lake Placid, New York. They had a beautiful relationship, akin to my own parents' one. After Harry's death, she moved to New York City. On each of my visits to the city, she and I would have dinner, go to the ballet, and enjoy her many friends of all ages there.

I adored Aunt Sister. One evening in 1961, she and I were sitting at the kitchen table in my parents' home in Louisville.

"Mary Ann," she said, "I have breast cancer and will not likely be able to go back to New York. I want you to know how much I love you and how grateful I am that your parents have welcomed me so warmly into their home and will care for me."

She was not maudlin, filled with self-pity, or anger.

"I have had an interesting life in New York in spite of the loss of the love of my life, Harry Huling. We enjoyed a perfect marriage. I never considered another relationship after his death."

"I love you also, Aunt Sister," I told her. "You are a role model for me. If Bill and I have children, we are going to name our first daughter Elizabeth Strong Connell after you."

Aunt Sister died in our family home on East Main Street in Louisville on December 27, 1961. She was a devout Episcopalian. There was not an Episcopal Church in Louisville. We held her funeral at the First Presbyterian Church and buried her next to my grandfather in the family plot in Louisville.

Bill and I kept the promise to Aunt Sister and had our first child baptized at St. George's Church in Clarksdale on June 16, 1963, and named her Elizabeth Strong Connell.

Elizabeth was a beautiful baby. All of Tankie's friends, as well as friends of Bill's and mine, came to Rena Lara daily to see her and exclaim how beautiful she was and how much she looked like Bill.

"Connell through and through," they would say. "The image of Billy."

Finally, Greenie McKee had heard enough of the Connell talk and complete omission of me and my family in the process.

"She looks like Kenneth to me," Greenie said, referring to our close friend Kenneth Williams. A hush fell over the room.

That ended the Connell look-alike conversations.

We chose Greenie and E'Lane Bobo as her godmothers; Kenneth Williams and Syd Sessions as her godfathers. Elizabeth wore the Connell family baptismal gown that her grandmother, Thankful Terrell "Tankie" Baugh Connell, had worn when she was baptized and that Bill and his siblings had worn when they were baptized. Tankie had preserved the gown, and after each baptism in which the gown was worn, she had embroidered in the lining of the gown the name of the baptized child.

Bill remained loyal to and interested in his college fraternity, Phi Delta Theta; he was a province president of the organization. His responsibil-

Jimmy Walker, Bill, and
Kenneth Williams, circa 1966

ities were to visit all the chapters in Mississippi, Tennessee, and Louisiana on an annual basis to review the activities of the chapters and be sure they were complying with national standards in all areas from recruitment to academics. I always accompanied him on these trips and enjoyed meeting many new friends. In addition to the campus chapter visits, Bill attended the annual conventions. Our first convention was held in Houston, Texas, in 1961. At that meeting, the Ole Miss chapter received the Founder's Day Award as the most outstanding chapter in the nation. Willis and Ed Connell, Bill's first cousins, received the Arthur R. Priest Award in 1960 and 1961, respectively, for being the most outstanding members in any chapter in the nation.

In 1964, we attended the Phi Delta Theta annual convention in Pasadena, California, accompanied by Clarksdale friends Sarah and Jimmy Walker and Kenneth Williams. We were in a bar in the hotel where the convention was taking place, when an attractive young couple at the table next to us began to talk with us about things all Southerners love to talk about; i.e., who you know from where, where you went to college, and such. Their names were Allister and Bill Estes from Nashville, Tennessee. Kenneth, Allister, and Bill Estes were all Vanderbilt graduates, so we struck up an immediate friendship.

Bill and I spent the weekend of the Ole Miss-Vanderbilt game, October 24-26, 1964, with the Esteses. The drive to Nashville was spectacular with all the hardwood trees showing their finest fall foliage. We stayed with Allister's parents, Mr. and Mrs. McDougall, because at that time Allister and Bill had two young children in a starter home and there was not enough room there for us. I made a pound cake to take to Mrs. McDougall as a hostess gift. The Esteses entertained us in high style with a tour of Belle Meade Mansion, a brunch in the McDougalls' home the day of the game, and an English breakfast at the Belle Meade Country Club after the Ole Miss and Vanderbilt game. We dined and danced to the music of Dean Hudson and his orchestra. *The Nashville Banner* reported the event, listing many members and their guests, among whom were "Mr. and Mrs. William Estes, Jr., and their guests, Mr. and Mrs. William C. Connell, Jr., of Rena Lara, Mississippi."

Nashville and the Delta had much in common – a graciousness in entertaining and welcoming of out-of-town guests. Allister and Bill came to Rena Lara to visit us the following year. We took them to see the levee along the Mississippi River, attended a party at the home of Nancy and Carter Stovall at Stovall, Mississippi, and drove the following day to Oxford to attend the Ole Miss-Vanderbilt game. Laura prepared a lavish feast for us to take in our basket to picnic from the trunk of our car in the Grove at Ole Miss. We had barely left Clarksdale, on our way to the game, before Allister and I started unpacking the fried chicken and began our pre-Grove snacking. Allister said the visit and the Delta culture were unlike anything she had ever seen.

Delta parties took on traditions of their own. For example, Tankie and Bill Connell, my in-laws, hosted an eggnog party each Christmas morning, which was attended by several hundred guests. Each Christmas evening, Nola and Andy Porter had a party. All the guests with children were exhausted by then, but never missed the party.

My in-laws had lovely friends who were kind, gracious, and accepting of me. I remember with especial fondness Nell Stribling, the mother of Jimmy and Sister Stribling. Sister was the wife of renowned portrait artist, Marshall Bouldin. For a wedding gift, Nell gave us a coffee table. When our daughter Elizabeth was two, Marshall painted an exquisite pastel of Elizabeth, which he gave Bill in exchange for Bill's photographing his four sons.

The Delta is virtually impossible to explain to people who are not from Mississippi. It's an idiosyncratic culture. At once warm and inviting; at another, agricultural and dependent, literally, on swings of the weather. It is filled with examples of gracious living and charm; it is also a place brimming with hardship and heartache — much of it hidden away by those who want to keep up appearances. But it was where my husband lived and I was beginning to feel like I might belong.

20

In 1964, I endured two more miscarriages, but by the spring of 1965, I was pregnant again and hopeful for another healthy child.

On Sunday, May 2, 1965, my parents went to Grenada Lake to fish, something they loved doing together. Trolling around the lake in their boat around 5:30 that afternoon, my mother heard my father shriek with pain, grab his chest and left arm, and then tumble over onto the bottom of the boat. She was terrified and started calling for help. Soon a couple in a nearby boat heard her and came to assist her. They pulled her boat to shore and called for help.

When the doctor arrived, he pronounced that my father had died from a massive heart attack.

Several friends from Louisville rushed to Grenada Lake and drove my mother home to Louisville.

My mother's world ended as the sun set over Grenada Lake that day. She never recovered from my father's death and the loss of their beautiful, passionate, and loving relationship.

My father's funeral service was held at the First Methodist Church of Louisville at 10:30 a.m. on May 4, 1965. The crowd overflowed the seating capacity of the church. In addition to a legend of friends from Louisville and the legal community, members of the Mississippi Legislature, former Gov. J.P. Coleman, and friends from Clarksdale attended the service.

My father's legal career was distinguished. He served as a special district attorney for the Fifth Judicial District, and a special chancellor for the Sixth Judicial District. He was president of the Winston County Bar Association, and a member of the Mississippi and American Bar Associations. He was president of the Louisville Business Men's Club, a member of the American Legion and the Veterans of Foreign Wars, as well as a member of the board of stewards and board of trustees of the First Methodist Church of Louisville. He served as a colonel on the staffs of former governors Fielding Wright, Hugh White, and J.P. Coleman. He served as chairman of the Mississippi Board of Bar Admissions for two years and was a member of the State Game and Fish Commission. He also served as attorney for the Board of Trustees of the Winston County Hospital and of the Louisville Housing and Airport boards. He was elected as a bar commissioner from the 5th Circuit Court District for the years 1964-65.

But what I remember most was the loving father he had been to me and to my brother, Billy, and the dedicated husband he was to my mother.

During the service, as Jerome Smith, the local high school principal, sang "In the Garden," I felt a feeling I'd experienced six times before. I didn't want to interrupt my father's service, but I feared I was suffering another miscarriage.

I rode with my mother and Bill to the Masonic Cemetery for my father's internment. He was laid to rest next to my grandfather, William Augustus Strong, Sr.; my brother, William Augustus Strong, III, (Billy); my uncle, Malcolm Whatley Strong (Uncle Mac); and my great aunt, Elizabeth Strong Huling (Aunt Sister).

At the conclusion of the graveside service, Bill returned to the Delta along with all the other Connell men to plant cotton.

My mother and I drove to her house. As soon we changed out of our funeral clothes, I told my mother, "I need to go to the hospital."

The day my father was buried, I lost twins.

I remained at the hospital in Louisville with my mother at my side. This miscarriage was much more difficult than the others. I was much further along with the twins.

On a Saturday, after my discharge from Winston County Hospital, my mother drove me back to Rena Lara. The drive was long and quiet. Collectively, mother and I had lost a husband, a father, two children, and two grandchildren in the course of two days.

When I returned home to Rena Lara, Bill met me in the dining room. He was wearing his work clothes — khaki pants and a white, cotton short-sleeve shirt. He looked distraught, on the verge of tears. He asked me to sit at our dining table with him.

"I've got something bad to tell you, Mary Ann," he said.

I couldn't imagine dealing with any more bad news.

"What?" I asked, reaching for his hand.

"Daddy has sold the Rena Lara place."

I could tell Bill was in shock. He had farmed the land for 13 years.

As a consolation, Mr. Connell had offered Bill the opportunity to farm the Baugh Plantation and some other land he owned, with Bill's brother Oscar. But we both knew that would not work. The brothers were very different and could never work together as had their father and uncle.

Bill's home place had just been sold to a physician from Memphis.

Bill was 38 years old; I was 27. We both felt lost. And neither of us knew what our future held.

V
Oxford

21

Bill and I began to explore our options.

We considered moving to Hawaii so Bill could work for Dole Pineapple.

Bill had loved being in the military, but he had been out for over ten years by this time and was almost 40, too old to rejoin.

Other than the military, Bill had worked for himself as a farmer and would not have adapted easily to working for someone else.

Nothing seemed to fall into place, to be a good fit. Bill, understandably, was apprehensive about our future. But I was not.

A year earlier, I had enrolled at Ole Miss to take courses that would enable me to obtain a teacher's license. I'd taken several correspondence courses over the course of the summer of 1965 and had driven every day during the fall 1965 semester to Oxford to take 15 hours in the School of Education. I loved being back in school and enjoyed my classes. There were several older students from the Delta area who were doing the same thing. We met each morning at 7:30 a.m. in a little park off Highway 6 in Marks, Mississippi, and carpooled the rest of the way.

We returned each day from Oxford to Clarksdale facing a blinding, sinking western sun.

Bill had a small, side photography business. He specialized in taking photographs of children and families in natural light — a relatively new concept.

As much as I had learned to love Clarksdale and the Delta, I realized that it was not going to work for us to continue to live there. Bill resented his brother Oscar and his father for selling the Rena Lara farm.

One day he said, "Why don't we move to Oxford? You can continue to go to school, and I can start a photography business there."

I smiled. That seemed to be the perfect solution.

We found a house we loved at the end of Phillip Road and paid $22,000 for it.

There was no mailbox and no house number, so Bill put up a mail box and declared the house number to be 16 Phillip Road. We had three small bedrooms and a tiny office. It had a garage that someday could be enclosed and turned it into an office and dark room for Bill's business.

Around this same time, Margaret and Robert Khayat moved to Oxford from Pascagoula, and Robert joined the faculty at the law school. Robert and I renewed our friendship upon their return to Oxford. Margaret was eight years younger. She and I had not known each other in college, but we became close friends after they moved into their Avent Acres home.

We shared the joys of young mothers in selecting Christmas toys, arranging play dates, talking about kindergarten, and agonizing over our children's holiday wear. During those days we and other young housewives saved the Quality Stamps we received when shopping at Larson's Big Star. We would paste the stamps into the stamp books all year until we had enough booklets to justify a trip to Memphis, Tennessee, to the Quality Stamp Store, where we would redeem our stamps for items such as bathroom scales or lamps.

On one such trip, Margaret and I were standing in the Quality Stamp store on Union Avenue, looking down into the glass counter trying to decide what we would trade our stamps for. The sales lady who was helping us looked up and said, "You are the most beautiful young woman I have ever seen."

"Well, thank you," I said.

"Oh no, honey, not you," she answered. "It is your friend I am talking about."

My ego was obviously bruised, but I traveled back to Oxford with Margaret. And we continued to visit the Quality Stamp store together year after year.

22

Shortly after Bill and I settled into our home on Phillip Road, I applied and was accepted into the graduate program in history, and I began taking classes in the fall semester of 1966.

The first course was historiography under Dr. Claire Marquette, who was married to Lena Mitchell from Louisville. The Marquettes were personal friends of my parents and took a special interest in me and in our family.

I enjoyed the classes I took in Tudor and Stuart England from Dr. Michael Landon. Dr. Landon was well-organized and well-versed in his area. Under his direction, I wrote a paper about the birth of James III and the suspicions on the part of English Protestants that Mary Beatrice, wife of Catholic James II, could not possibly be pregnant at the old age of 30. Rumor was rampant she was not pregnant at all, but that she had stuffed pillows under her clothing to make her appear to be with child.

When time for delivery of the baby arrived, Mary Beatrice advised James to summon those he wished to witness the birth to come to St. James' Palace, where she would deliver the child. When her labor began, she was in the room with the midwife and one other. She complained of being cold and asked to have the bed warmed. A warming pan of hot coals was brought into the room and placed in her bed. From this circumstance — simple but unusual in June — came the tale of the "spurious child," the "Warming-Pan Baby."

This supposed event led to the Glorious Revolution that brought Protestant William and Mary from the Netherlands to assume the Royal Throne.

During my first semester in graduate school, on October 24, 1966, Jimmy Walker called and said that he would be making a speech in Pontotoc, Mississippi, that evening at 7:00 on behalf of Senator Eastland's campaign for reelection to the U.S. Senate.

Jimmy wanted to drive over and spend the night with us after the political event was over. We were delighted, of course, because we always loved to spend time with Jimmy. As the night wore on and Jimmy did not arrive, I suggested we go to bed and leave the lights on for him because I had an 8:00 a.m. class the next morning.

Just as I was dozing off to sleep, I heard the phone ring and Bill cry out. "No, No, No!"

"What!?" I asked.

Bill turned to me and said, "It's Brad Dye. Jimmy lost control of his car in the rain on the Natchez Trace near Houston, Mississippi, crashed into a tree, and broke his neck." Bill paused. "Jimmy's dead."

Bill cried with deep anguish, something I had never seen him do. He cried for my friend who had become his. I think he cried for all the suffering I had lived through and for Sarah, whom he had come to love.

I was devastated. I loved Jimmy like a brother and could not imagine life without his exuberant personality and zest for life.

The next morning, we drove to Lambert, Mississippi, to the Delta home of Jimmy's parents, Dr. and Mrs. James P. Walker. Sarah arrived shortly thereafter holding a picture of Jimmy.

Their daughter, Sarah, my goddaughter, was one year old. Jimmy was 31 at the time of his death.

Jimmy's funeral was held in the Methodist Church in Lambert, with hundreds in attendance. Not only was the church filled to capacity, but so were the grounds surrounding the church. Jimmy was beloved by so many.

The Commercial Appeal ran a news story with the caption, "Eastland, Foe Halt Campaign to Mourn Loss." The article described Jimmy as "a personable young attorney and state representative from Marks, Mississippi, and one of the brightest young political stars."

Jimmy was buried in the cemetery south of Lambert near a beautiful magnolia tree. On every occasion I have traveled past that spot, I have always stopped to reflect on the depth of our friendship and how much Jimmy meant to me.

23

The university required a thesis for the M.A. in history.

"Why don't you write your thesis on something alive and interesting in your own back yard — like the Peabody Hotel?" Bill suggested.

He went on. "The history of the hotel reflects the history of the mid-South region over nearly a hundred-year period."

I couldn't help but wonder if Bill was suggesting this topic because of all the partying he had engaged in at the Peabody prior to our marriage.

Dr. John Moore, and his wife, Margaret, were excellent teachers and personal friends. Dr. Moore, my thesis director, was a visionary who found the topic interesting. With his support and guidance, and Bill's encouragement, I began work on the project.

Every Tuesday for almost two years, I drove to Memphis to conduct my research in the Cossitt Library, at the *Commercial Appeal*, and also at the Peabody Hotel. I interviewed dozens of people who had built or worked at the Peabody. Most of those Tuesdays, I had cream of celery soup and cornbread for lunch in downtown Memphis at The Little Tea Room.

Bill was supportive of my graduate studies and frequently accompanied me to Memphis to interview hotel employees and Memphians, who loved their Peabody.

These were good times. We were loving living in Oxford, making friends, and rejoicing in the birth on August 16, 1968, of our daughter, Stella Garrett Connell, whom we named in honor of Bill's grandmother, Stella Garrett Baugh, and his sister, Stella Connell Salmon. We asked Sarah Longino Walker and Martha Jane Howell to be her godmothers; Harvey Henderson and Bob Bobo to be her godfathers. Stella arrived in this world a happy, smiling, healthy baby.

On September 14, 1969, our third daughter, Mary Ann, arrived and was a sweet, loving, little girl. Bill insisted that we name her for me. We chose Mollie Morse and Freemie Stone as her godmothers; and Graham

Bramlett and Bill Heaton as her godfathers. Both Stella and Mary Ann were baptized at St. Peter's Episcopal Church in Oxford by our rector and close friend, The Rev. Don M. Morse.

In addition to my graduate studies, I was deeply involved in the Episcopal Church as well as community activities.

One evening after dinner in 1969, the phone rang at our home on Phillip Road in Oxford.

Bill answered it. He listened intently for a moment.

"Howorth," he said, "have you lost your mind?"

Dr. Beckett Howorth was medical director at the Oxford Lafayette County Hospital. He was trying to convince Bill of something.

"No," Bill said, "Mary Ann cannot serve on the hospital board!"

Beckett continued to try to persuade Bill.

"What are you thinking of putting a woman on the hospital board?" Bill reiterated. "And, no you do not need to talk with her about this because she is not going to be on your board."

Dr. Beckett and Mary Hartwell Howorth were close personal friends of ours with whom we had shared many delightful evenings, but to Bill, Dr. Howorth's request was a step too far.

Two weeks later, the phone rang again.

Bill answered and a sense of *deja vu* came over me. "Morse," Bill said, "this is crazy. Are you trying to ruin the church?" Rev. Don Morse was calling to ask me to serve on the vestry of the church. "No, Mary Ann is not going to do that," Bill said. "It is ridiculous of you to ask!"

Bill was convinced that no woman, especially me, should serve on the vestry. In his view, the vestry was a group reserved for men.

24

When I completed my thesis, Dr. Moore accepted it and awarded me the grade of "A." I passed my orals and received my master's degree in history on January 25, 1971. As a graduation gift, Bill and the girls gave me a small silver tray. Engraved on the tray was the date and a message: "Welcome back Mama."

Shortly thereafter radio station WREG in Memphis asked permission to have my thesis read over the radio each evening at 7:00 p.m. for several weeks. My thesis beamed over the mid-South and received accolades. Much of the credit for that happy time goes to Bill's imagination and encouragement, and to the courage of Dr. Moore to think outside the traditional confines of academia.

I then began work on a master's degree in library science. Dr. Ellis Tucker and Myra Macon were excellent professors in this field. I read many books in children's literature, such as *Charlotte's Web*," that were mainstays of my own children's literary childhood.

Much of my time during 1973 was spent in the John D. Williams Library. The smell of a library is one of life's joys to me. Walking among the stacks, looking at the thousands of titles of books that represent knowledge and scholarship thrilled me. I was fortunate to have a carrel that looked north on the sixth floor toward the dormitories that housed student-athletes. I felt like I belonged to that space and spent hours studying there.

I wrote my thesis on "Educational and Job Opportunities for Law Librarians." I received my library Science master's degree in May 1973.

Our fourth daughter, Jane Danzey Connell, was born on July 26, 1973. She was a pretty, happy baby. We named her for my Aunt Jane and for my mother, who was called Danzey by most of her friends. I wish that we had called Jane both names.

My Aunt Jane was my mother's half-sister. They had the same father, but different mothers. Aunt Jane taught math and science, as well as drama at Jacksonville High School in Jacksonville, Alabama. Her husband, my Uncle Reuben Self, was a professor at Jacksonville State University. They were powerful influences in my life. Both were intelligent, well-read, highly energized, and fiercely loyal Democrats. They were well informed on current events and expected me to be so also during the weeks each summer I spent in their home. They inspired me with their intellectual curiosity and devotion to their ideals of what a truly inclusive democracy should be.

They both had a strong sense of family loyalty and responsibility. They were with my mother when Billy died. When my parents hosted a reception in Louisville for Bill and me after we were married, they were there.

Their daughter Jane Self Burnham was as accomplished as her parents. She received her master's degree in music education from Columbia University and was an excellent pianist. Her husband, Pat, was one of Alabama's finest trial attorneys, a member of the American College of Trial Lawyers, and a member of the Alabama legislature until he took a strong stand against Governor George Wallace, which ended his career in politics.

On one occasion, Pat, along with a medical malpractice attorney from Birmingham, represented a local pediatric physician from Anniston, Alabama, who was being sued for using a product on an injured six-year-old little boy who had been left brain-damaged and with numerous serious physical problems.

At the end of putting on his case-in-chief, the plaintiff's attorney called as his last witness the child, assisted him to the witness stand, and asked him: "Will you sing a song for the jury?"

The child was barely able to walk or to speak, but he loved to sing. He sat in the jury box alone and in a sweet, clear voice sang:

"Jesus loves me, this I know."

There was not a dry eye in the courtroom.

Following the song, Pat turned to his co-counsel and said:

"Somebody better get their checkbook out now."

The jury returned a multi-million dollar verdict for the plaintiff against the manufacturer in short order, but found the physician free of liability.

In the fall of 1973, I enrolled in a torts class in law school. I kept it a secret from Bill.

25

After Bill's conversations with Dr. Howorth (about my serving on the hospital board) and with Don Morse (about my serving on the vestry), I knew he would never approve of my going to law school.

But I didn't let that stop me.

Robert Khayat was my professor, a strange experience for both of us since we had been undergraduate students together at Ole Miss and were friends. I was now sitting in the second-story lecture room in Farley Hall under his tutelage. Professor Khayat assigned a casebook and told us to consider *Prosser's The Law of Torts* to be our hornbook. (In United States legal education, a hornbook is a one-volume treatise, written for law students on subjects typically covered by law school courses.)

I enjoyed his class from the first moment. Professor Khayat was a gifted teacher. He was always prepared and explained the concepts of tort law and the cases in a manner easy to understand and apply. All the students in the class held him in high regard. We could not wait until the next class, when Professor Khayat would take us through the four elements of a negligence cause of action, intentional torts, or products liability in ways that we understood and enjoyed.

He made the classic *Palsgraf v. Long Island Railroad Company* case so clear and real that I thought I had been on the Atlantic Avenue platform of the train station with Helen Palsgraf as she was on her way to Rockaway Beach.

In Professor Khayat's torts class, we also learned that the conduct of a person in a torts case is measured by the standard of what a reasonably prudent person in similar circumstances would do. The mythical person, against whom all of our conduct would be measured, was referred to as the "Reasonable Man." Law school students then knew the "Reasonable Man" had to be Professor Khayat.

On a Saturday afternoon in October of 1973, a friend and fellow law school classmate, George Fair from Louisville, came to our home to visit.

We sat in Bill's office and talked.

George turned to me and said, "Mary Ann, how are you liking our torts class?"

My heart sank.

"What are you talking about?" Bill exclaimed. "Torts is a law class."

I knew Bill would never have agreed for me to go to law school. That did not fit the mold of the wife he or those of his generation expected. Roles for women were clearly defined in those days, and they did not encompass entering male-dominated professions or serving on male-dominated boards.

My sins had found me out. I had deceived Bill and my family. I had enrolled in law school and kept it a secret. I was caught and had to confess.

Bill was furious.

I kept my opinion to myself, but I did not believe Bill was acting like the reasonable man.

The Connell family, circa 1973

26

Law school was a different experience for me than for most of my classmates. I had four children — one a newborn baby — and many responsibilities unrelated to the study of law.

I was a Girl Scout leader, taught Sunday School, entertained and attended social functions with my husband, just as I had done before going to law school.

I knew maintaining this balance was the only way that my law school studies would be accepted, or even tolerated, by Bill and some of our friends.

There were not many women in law school in the early 1970s, but there were some very capable ones. I had great respect for Allan Alexander and Debbie Bell. They were younger than I and much smarter. I admired the way they conducted themselves as women and professionals. They were not intimidated by the men around them, neither were they aggressive and overbearing to prove a point. They earned the respect of all students and faculty by being who they were: competent, gracious, and intelligent women.

My closest friend and colleague during my law school days was Duke Goza. He and I had attended Ole Miss together as undergraduate students. After graduation, Duke married Elizabeth Stansell and ran the grain elevator near Ruleville, Mississippi. After six years of that, Elizabeth and Duke moved to Oxford, and he began law school.

The friendship Duke and I shared deepened in law school when we were assigned to be moot court partners and together wrote our brief and argued the case assigned to us by the moot court board — *Johnny Firefly v. Faultless Light Company.*

Our facts were these: Johnny Firefly, twelve years old, was walking home from school when he saw a light pole of Faultless Light Company. Johnny, 5 feet 2 inches tall, climbed onto a wall surrounding the pole, and by standing on his tiptoes, was able to reach the first climbing rung of the pole. He climbed the pole and, holding onto a rung with one hand, reached out with the other hand for one of the wires. Upon touching the high voltage line, Johnny received a severe electrical shock, which knocked him to the ground. He suffered severe burns over his arms and face, lost two fingers, and was hospitalized for six weeks.

We were successful at trial and on appeal in bringing the facts of our case within the boundaries of the attractive nuisance doctrine by showing that Faultless Company knew its power pole was in a place where children were likely to trespass while walking home from school; the wires strung from the pole posed a high risk of danger; Johnny was too young to appreciate the danger; the cost to the light company by removing the low-climbing rungs on the pole was slight by comparison to the risk to Johnny; and the company failed to take reasonable care for Johnny's safety.

Bill brought our ten-year-old daughter, Elizabeth, to attend the oral argument in the moot court room in Farley Hall.

Duke and I were both nervous, but we apparently did fine because we won. We acted as if we had received a unanimous verdict from the U.S. Supreme Court.

Later in law school, I met Diann Coleman. We took federal jurisdiction together under Jim Zirkle. He was one of the Yale professors brought in to help raise the academic standing of the law school. I sensed Diann understood the subtleties and intricacies of Ex Parte Young and the Erie Doctrine, both of which were confusing to me.

I asked Diann if we could study together. She agreed and came to our home on Phillip Road to go over the Erie Doctrine with me repeatedly until I finally understood it. She then invited me to come to her home, where we sat in her living room and plodded through Ex Parte Young until I finally understood it too.

Diann was older than most students. She was closer to my age and had children at home, too. But Diann already had a group of friends with whom she studied, and they had a good time. When she told them she was going to study with me for two courses, they advised her against it.

"She is no fun," one of them said.

"She won't gossip about any of the professors or other students," another one told her.

I had some outstanding professors in law school, among whom was Cliff Hodge, who taught income taxation, a course in which I had little interest at the beginning. Cliff made the course so interesting that when it was over, I wished that I could have taken it again. Parham Williams was also a great teacher. He made the laws and rules of criminal procedure interesting and alive. Bill Champion did the same with wills and estates. Don Frugé taught estate and gift taxation and wills and trust drafting from a practical perspective. He knew the intricacies of estate taxation and prepared his students to draft wills and trusts that would stand the tests of time. Professor Bradley taught workers' compensation from a practical standpoint, which would prove to be invaluable.

As law school progressed and I was able to prove to Bill I could fulfill my role as wife, mother, hostess, and participant in the community, he softened. He started telling me how proud he was of what I was doing. He became downright supportive. He would take one or more of our girls with him as he traveled on his photography assignments around the southeast, especially during the days preceding my final exams. This allowed me rare moments when I could sit quietly in our home and study without interruption.

When grades were posted on the bulletin board on the first floor of Farley Hall, Bill would gather the girls together, and the six of us would make the trip to view my grades from the previous semester.

When my grades were good, he would give them the cue and they would all shout out "Good job, Mama," and celebrate with me.

I graduated from law school on May 26, 1977. The ceremony was held in Meek Hall.

As a graduation gift, Bill gave me a coin holder with "Mary Ann Connell, Attorney at Law, May 26, 1977" on the case, which contained a coin for each of our birthdays: a silver dollar for his birth year (1926); a half

Stella and Bill on a photography trip

27

After I graduated from law school, Grady Tollison and Robert Khayat offered me a position as an associate with their law firm, Holcomb, Dunbar, Connell, Merkel, Tollison, and Khayat.

On May 31, 1977, I arrived early at The Thompson House on the Oxford Square. That same morning, at about 7:30, a man dressed in overalls walked in.

"I need to see a lawyer," he said.

"I am a lawyer," I told him. "I will be glad to help you."

He stared at me. "You didn't hear me right," he said. "I don't need a woman. I need a lawyer."

I told him, again I was a lawyer.

"Are you married?" he asked.

"Yes, I am," I answered, wondering where this conversation was going.

"Do you have children?"

"Yes," I said, "I have four daughters."

"Then you are living in sin."

I told him I was unaware that sin included women working.

"The Lord meant for women to stay at home and take care of their husband and children," he said, "not out here calling themselves lawyers."

This was not how I thought my first day on my job as an attorney would begin.

"Where are the men?" he asked.

I said they had not arrived.

He retrieved his pocket watch from his overalls and looked at it carefully.

"It's 7:30 a.m.," he said, "The work day is half over and there is not a man in here. Where are they?" he asked.

"I am a lawyer," I repeated. "I am willing to help you. If you do not want to work with me, you can walk around the Square until you find a man you like."

He said he was too busy for that, so he reluctantly sat with me and discussed his concerns, protesting the entire time that he never thought he would live to see the day he would discuss his business with a woman.

I would soon discover that my new client was not the only person in Oxford unaccustomed to working with female attorneys.

Grady and Robert were both fine lawyers and teachers. Each man educated me in the practice of law, but in different ways. Robert was a born teacher. He taught me how to do title work, incorporate a business, and draft contracts.

Grady was a brilliant litigator. He was not a teacher in the traditional sense, but he instructed me by example and by giving me opportunities to question witnesses, prepare jury instructions, participate in conferences, and handle a number of matters on my own.

Our firm had a trial scheduled in circuit court during a period when Grady was particularly pressed for time.

"Mary Ann," he said, "walk across the street and try the case."

I was prepared because I had accompanied him on many different trials.

I walked into the courtroom, sat at counsel's table with our client, and announced we were ready to proceed.

The judge called me to the bench and asked if I intended to try this case without Mr. Tollison.

"Yes, your honor."

"Mrs. Connell," he said, "you don't need to be here. You need to go home. Women do not belong in the courtroom."

"I am sorry that you do not want me here," I said," but I am here to stay… and there will soon be many more like me."

"That's exactly what I am afraid of," he responded.

During this period, I often thought about my cousin Jane and the summer days I spent in my Aunt Jane and Uncle Reuben's home. Hanging on the wall in Jane's room on West Mountain Avenue in Jacksonville, Alabama, was a framed version of a poem written by J.P. McEnvoy in 1924, "If For Girls," inspired by Rudyard Kipling's renowned 1910 poem "If" [for boys].

If you can hear the whispering about you,
And never yield to deal in whispers, too;
If you can bravely smile when loved ones doubt you,
And never doubt, in turn, what loved ones do;
If you can keep a sweet and gentle spirit
In spite of fame and fortune, rank or place,
And though you win your goal or only near it,
Can win with poise or lose with equal grace;

If you meet with Unbelief, believing,
And hallow in your heart a simple Creed,
If you can meet Deception, undeceiving,
And learn to look to God for all you need;
If you can be what girls should be to mothers;
Chums in joy and comrades in distress,
And be unto others as you'd have the others
Be unto you – no more and yet no less;

If you can keep within your heart the power
To say that firm, unconquerable "No";
If you can brave a present shadowed hour
Rather than yield to build a future woe;
If you can love, yet not let loving master,
But keep yourself within your own self's clasp,

And not let dreaming lead you to disaster,
Nor pity's fascination lose your grasp.

If you can lock your heart on confidences,
Nor ever needlessly in turn confide;
If you can put behind all pretenses
Of mock humility or foolish pride;
If you can keep the simple, homely virtue
Of walking right with God – then have no fear
That anything in all the world can hurt you –
And – which is more – you'll be a Woman, dear.

28

Grady continued to send me to courtroom after courtroom to argue motions and represent clients. On one of those occasions, when the case was scheduled out of town, I stopped at the office to pick up the file. I was running late. I parked my lime green 1979 Ford LTD on North Lamar in a spot next to our office. I left the car unlocked and the keys in the ignition. I ran in, grabbed the file, and rushed back outside.

My car was gone.

My daughters, who hated the ugly car, secretly hoped it would never be found. But two weeks later, the police located the car in Holly Springs, Mississippi, along with the seventh-grade student who had stolen it.

The young man — who had skipped school one day and noticed the keys in the ignition — had also sold all the clothes I had in the trunk. According to the police, he sold them for gas money.

The officers brought him back to Oxford, arrested him, and, because of his age, insisted that he come to my office and apologize — not only for stealing my car, but also for selling all the clothes he found in the trunk — before sending him to youth court.

He walked into my office and stood in my doorway.

"I am sorry I took your car," he mumbled.

I accepted his apology.

"But you owe me $25," he added.

I didn't understand.

"After I sold your clothes," he explained, "I still didn't have enough money to buy gas and oil." Then he added, "You don't have a very nice car either. I didn't enjoy driving it."

At every turn, it seemed, I was being critiqued. But one spot was a safe haven, as it has always been — the classroom.

While I practiced with Grady and Robert, I also taught a legal bibliography and writing class at the University of Mississippi Law School. More than 350 students and I met in the moot court room on the second floor of Farley Hall.

Maintaining class order and decorum was difficult because of the large number of students. The class was not as exciting as some of the other classes, such as torts, criminal law, and constitutional law. To make matters worse, the class met from 4:30-6:30 p.m.

There were some exceptionally good students in the class. In particular, I remember Barry Cannada writing a legal memorandum so nearly perfect I could not find a single space on any page in which to make a correction.

Four gregarious, attractive young men sat near the back of the room in the middle section. The four friends seemed to be more interested in socializing and flirting with the female students than they were in learning the details of the Blue Book or how to write a legal memorandum or brief.

After a particularly frustrating class, I walked to the back of the classroom and stood in front of the four young law students. I gave them my sternest expression. Their smiles temporarily disappeared.

"You fellows," I said, shaking my finger and raising an eyebrow, "have got to get serious about what you are doing or you will never succeed in the practice of law." I paused for dramatic effect. "Or elsewhere."

The four first-year students nodded.

I stood before them for a moment making eye contact with each one — Mike Mills, Ronnie Musgrove, Roger Wicker, and John Grisham — hoping the lesson might sink in.

Then I turned and walked away, wondering if any of them would heed my advice.

Another one of my law students, Mr. Weinischske, approached me after class with a problem. He and his wife were renting an apartment in a complex on University Avenue owned by a local corporation. They found a small house to rent in Avent Acres, another area of town popular with young law student couples, and went to the manager of the apartments to give notice that they planned to move and wanted to give their one week's notice as required by law since they were on a month-to-month lease. They asked the manager to inspect their apartment and refund their $75.00 deposit.

"We do not return students' deposits," the manager said.

"But the law says that you must refund our deposit unless we have damaged the apartment," Mr. Weinischske told him.

"I don't care what the law says," the manager responded. "We are not refunding your deposit."

Mr. Weinischske went to the law school, found the volume of the Mississippi Code dealing with landlord-tenant relationships, and, accompanied by a classmate, returned to the corporate offices of the apartment complex.

"I have brought the volume of the Code to show you the law regarding returning of damage deposits," Mr. Weinischske told the manager.

The manager of the complex took the Code and threw it into the trash can.

"That is what I think of the law in this area," he said. "So, get out of here. I am not refunding your deposit."

My student came to me for help. I told him that I knew the attorney for the corporation and would place a call on his behalf. I was certain the attorney would talk sense into his client and have him refund my student's deposit.

"Mary Ann," the attorney for the complex told me, "you need to stay out of this. We are not going to refund deposits of students no matter what the Code says."

I was astounded.

"And, furthermore," he continued, "If you bother me any more about this, I am going to have Mr. Weinischske kicked out of law school."

"Mr. Weinsichske" I said, "Give me a check for $25.00 so that I can legally be your attorney, and we are going to sue the corporation."

He gave me the check, and I filed the complaint seeking reimbursement of the $75.00 deposit. In addition, I asked for punitive damages.

In the meantime, I asked Mr. Weinischke to take a number of his law school friends to view his apartment and take pictures of its condition. They did and found it to be immaculate. Everything was spotless. The holes in the wall where pictures had been hung were filled with spackling compound. The apartment was in perfect condition. The photographs and the testimony of the law students supported that.

Trial started before the same judge who had told me to "go home because women were going to ruin the practice of law."

I called Mr. Weinischke, his wife, and several law students as witnesses. I introduced the photographs, and then called the owner of the corporation to establish his worth for purposes of establishing punitive damages.

I asked him to review his corporate tax returns with me.

"I can't," he responded.

"And why not?" I asked.

"Because I did not bring my glasses," he said.

He was a terrible witness who offended the jury and me.

At the end of the trial, the jury deliberated about thirty minutes. They returned with a verdict for the plaintiff (Mr. Weinischke) in the amount of $75.00 (his deposit) and $25,000 in punitive damages.

Associate U.S. Attorney Al Moreton was on the jury. He told me he had to use his influence to keep the jury from awarding many times more in punitive damages because they were so outraged at the conduct of the defendant.

In my early days of law practice, there were not many lawyers in Oxford. Cooperation and assistance were key words around the Oxford Square. We all helped each other. If you did not know how to do something, you called another lawyer around town who did that type work and he, and sometimes she, helped you. Civility and cordiality reigned.

Title work was a world all its own. Charles Walker was an expert in this field and always remained gracious and kind about helping those of us who were not as competent as he in the area of searching land records. Diann Coleman had a true affinity for searching titles and became fascinated with each transaction. She spent hours in the courthouse with Charles lugging down those big, heavy books to trace land transactions.

Most lawyers in Oxford then did not bill by the hour or keep time of their work. They charged what they thought was fair and reasonable. When Jack Dunbar, one of Mississippi's most outstanding lawyers, moved to Oxford from his Clarksdale home office to work with Grady, Robert, and me, he changed our method of billing and insisted that we keep detailed records of everything we did every day. We billed on a one-sixth of an hour basis, like city firms did. We all resisted this method of billing and time-keeping, but I gradually adjusted to it, and it became a life-long habit with me.

In addition to Grady, Robert, and Jack, Holcomb Dunbar had other outstanding lawyers. Ronny Roberts joined us in 1978; Dan Webb in 1979; Guy Gillespie and Allan Alexander (later federal magistrate judge) in 1980. They were all excellent lawyers, and it was an exciting place to work.

We had some outstanding judges during those days as well. I recall especially United States District Court Judges William Keady, author of *All Rise*; Judge Orma Smith; and Chancery Court Judge Glenn Fant. These men enhanced the quality of law practice in Oxford.

Robert Khayat and I shared the services of legal assistant Norma White, wife of Oxford's chief of police, Billy White. Norma was a perfectionist and a stern taskmaster. She held both Robert and me to the line on everything, and she contributed to making us better lawyers, certainly in the area of attention to detail.

As for my first client, the gentleman with the pocketwatch and over-alls who never dreamed of telling his business problems to a woman, he and I worked together for five years. After our business came to an end, he stopped by the office early one morning dragging a large croaker sack alongside him.

"You did good work for me," he said. "Although you are still living in sin. I'm gonna miss you. I went coon hunting last night, and I've brought you a sack of coons I killed as a thank you gift for the good work you've done for me."

I thanked him. He handed me the sack of coons. Then he left.

I stood outside the front door of our office holding a sack of dead coons. About that time, a young Oxford Police Department officer walked by, noticed my dilemma, and took the coons off my hands.

29

While I spent many hours at the law office and in the courtroom, I also loved afternoons, evenings, and weekends with my family and neighbors on Phillip Road.

Bill was enjoying his photography business. It was growing rapidly. It involved a great deal of travel to other states where Bill, through his national involvement with Phi Delta Theta, had representatives who arranged appointments for him to take pictures of families in natural light.

He frequently took one of our girls with him, and sometimes I went. We had interesting travel adventures and made friends with his representatives and clients all over the South.

Bill wrote a book titled *Part-Time Photography for Money: A Guide to Supplementary Income with a Camera*, which was self-published by The Four Daughters Press (his idea).

It contained dozens of excellent pointers on how to take group pictures, individual portraits, family pictures (with and without the family pet), and how to make money from the pictures. He sold hundreds of copies of the books and saved one for each of our four daughters.

We once traveled to Camden, South Carolina, where Bill photographed members of the William F. Buckley family. I enjoyed a delightful relationship with Mr. Buckley's mother. On another trip to Camden, Bill took our daughter Stella with him as he photographed members of one of the DuPont families.

After the photographs were taken, the DuPonts invited Bill and Stella in for a visit in their home.

The conversation wandered to traveling with children and how expensive it could be. Stella went to the car and brought inside a cheap suitcase with bumper stickers and school pennants pasted all over it.

"Mr. Dupont," Stella explained, "this is the food suitcase."

The Connell family and Mimi, circa 1977

She told Mr. Dupont that the "food suitcase" contained a water boiler and several cans of spaghetti, soup, chicken and dumplings, which, Stella explained, she and her father heated up in the motel room to save money.

Mr. DuPont told Stella he thought that was a brilliant idea and proclaimed that he intended to adopt that practice in the future when traveling with his children.

Among our closest friends during these Phillip Road years were Mollie and Don Morse. Mollie and Don had four children. Their daughter Cynthia and our daughter Elizabeth were the same age and spent many hours in each other's homes. We frequently had the Morses for Easter Sunday dinner and captured — in home movies — all of the Morse and Connell children in the front yard on Phillip Road hunting for Easter eggs.

Across the street on Phillip Road lived three-year-old Brian Harvey. He and Jane were exactly the same age. They immediately became friends and wanted to play together all the time. They both had "Big Wheels," a tricycle-type riding toy with big rear wheels, which they could ride to the edge of their driveways and talk back and forth across the street with each other. To their consternation, they were forbidden to cross the street without supervision so they just parked their "Big Wheels" at the end of their respective driveways and made silly faces at each other, talking and laughing back and forth.

Further up Phillip Road, closer to College Hill Road, lived Laura and John Robin Bradley and their children, Mark and Claire. Mark was smart, a great tennis player, and the hero of the street. Claire and Elizabeth were the same age and good friends. Laura and I became good friends. I had then and have now great respect for her intelligence and used to say that if it were not for Laura and *Time* magazine, I would not know what I would think about many different issues.

On Phillip Road, the children played in the big ditch beside our house. They would swing across the ditch on vines hanging from the trees, walk across the ditch on a fallen tree high above the water, and crawl through the culvert that ran under Phillip Road to the other side of the street where the Aldersons and Harveys lived. I never gave thought to how many mosquitoes and snakes were probably sharing their playground.

Everyone in Oxford was excited when the city acquired a bug-spraying machine. The truck would periodically drive up and down the street, spraying a heavy, cloudy fume of poison that would kill the mosquitoes. But no one was more excited than the neighborhood children, who loved to get on their bikes and follow the bug-spraying truck.

As with most young married couples, however, life was not always bliss.

One day I returned from Memphis after a day of shopping with friends and could not wait to try my new dress on for Bill to see.

Before going to put on the dress to model for Bill, I removed a hot spinach casserole from the oven so it could cool.

I put on the new dress — it had an argyle pattern of brown and pine green — and returned to the kitchen.

"How do you like it?" I asked Bill.

"It looks like something my grandmother would wear," he responded rudely.

I picked up the hot spinach casserole and slammed it down on the counter. The casserole dish broke with such force that spinach splashed up and covered the ceiling.

I ran out of the kitchen crying and furious.

A few minutes later, the children came running inside, just as I was climbing a ladder to clean the spinach off the ceiling.

"Why did Mama throw the spinach all over the ceiling?" one of them said.

"What a mess!" another one laughed.

It is a wonder I didn't throw the casserole over all of them.

I am slow to anger, but when I do get mad, I get really, really mad.

Shortly after I started the practice of law, my mother —"Mimi" as our daughters called her — sold her home on East Main Street in Louisville and moved to Oxford.

The move was painful for her because her life with my father in Louisville had been so wonderful. We looked at houses, but we did not find one that seemed right so we settled on her moving into an apartment at the corner of University Avenue and South 9th Street. The location close to campus and to the Square was perfect and the apartment attractive, but it was a mistake. We should have bought a small house with a yard, because my mother loved the out-of-doors and would have been happier in a house.

She adored Dave Fair. Dave grew up in Louisville, and the Fairs were a prominent family and long-time, multi-generational family friends. He came to see her frequently and enjoyed watching the Boston Red Sox and Atlanta Braves with her. Frequently, he brought his son Deck with him, whom she also adored.

My mother made many friends in Oxford, played bridge frequently, and was active in the Methodist Church. She enjoyed the girls coming over and getting to attend their school functions. She would take them shopping and buy them nice clothes, but I worried whether we made the right decision by moving her to Oxford and taking her away from the place she had loved, a decision faced by many with aging parents.

30

The city of Oxford annexed the St. Andrews Circle and Price Hill subdivisions in 1978. To obtain court approval of the annexation, the city represented to the chancery court that it would provide all city services to newly annexed areas within a reasonable time, including water and sewer. In turn, the annexed areas would pay city taxes in exchange for the services the city would provide.

After three years, the city still had not provided sewer and water services to these areas.

During the 1980-81 school year, raw sewage began to seep into the yards of homeowners in both the St. Andrews and Price Hill areas. Residents were appalled as toilet paper and other evidences of raw sewage covered their lawns and flowed into the streets of these neighborhoods. Children were forced to walk through these areas to meet the school bus and then tracked the sewage onto the buses.

Many residents of both areas called the mayor's office to complain. They also called upon their alderperson representing this area of Oxford but were brushed off at every turn with a promise of, "We will get to it when we have the money to install the sewer lines." Initially, this was the repeated response, and it went on for months.

The situation became unacceptable and unhealthy. I went home for lunch one day and saw raw sewage in the street. I called Bill at his camera shop and asked him to come home with his camera and walk the St. Andrews and Price Hill areas with me and photograph the yards where the sewage was evident.

He did and developed the prints. The images were disgusting.

I called the State Board of Health and explained the situation.

They said they would send two representatives to Oxford to review our neighborhoods to inspect the situation to see if it was as bad as I indicated and the pictures revealed. They came, visited the areas of my complaint, and confirmed that the sewage situation was critical.

Shortly thereafter, I went to Leslie's Drug Store one afternoon and presented the pictures to John Leslie, Oxford's mayor at the time.

Mayor Leslie was drinking coffee in the back of the store with a group of men, including my husband, Bill.

"Mr. Mayor," I said, "the city has to correct this situation now."

He turned to Bill. "Connell," he said, "you need to do something about your wife. She is really getting on my nerves."

"Mr. Mayor," I said, anger building in my voice, "you have the photographs, and, you have the reports from the representatives of the State Department of Health. By this time tomorrow, you will have petitions signed by most residents of St. Andrews and Price Hills subdivisions asking the city to provide that which it is under a duty to provide." I paused. "After that, you will have one day to begin constructing sewage lines in the St. Andrews and Price Hill subdivisions or these petitions, photographs, and reports will go to Washington. Then your troubles will really begin."

"Mary Ann," he said, "You stay out of Price Hill. You will really stir up trouble if you get those folks involved."

Price Hill was a black neighborhood.

"I will go to every home in Price Hill," I said. "This is not an idle threat. We deserve better."

The following day, I delivered the signed petitions to the mayor, along with a final one-day ultimatum.

The following afternoon, construction crews were in both Price Hill and St. Andrews subdivisions installing sewer lines.

The mayor and I drew swords over the sewer situation, but we remained friends.

From that day on, whenever he saw me, Mayor Leslie called me "The Sewer Queen."

In early 1982, Bill began to feel tired and thought he had the flu. Like so many men, he refused to go to the doctor until I harassed him into going to see Dr. Mitt Hobbs, a new young doctor who was treating our family. Dr. Hobbs told Bill he did not have the flu and needed to have tests to determine what might be the cause of his general malaise.

Dr. Hobbs ordered a biopsy of Bill's liver, and then he met with Bill and me in his hospital room on the night of the Ole Miss-Vanderbilt five-overtime basketball game.

"I am not an oncologist, and you should get an opinion from a physician in this area," he said. "But I can tell you from the results of the biopsy and my other examinations, the future does not hold a bright prognosis for Bill."

He referred us to an oncologist in Memphis, where more testing revealed a tumor on Bill's liver. It was malignant.

The doctor sent us home to await surgery.

We returned to Memphis for the surgery two weeks later. The doctor told us he had never seen a patient lose weight and coloring as rapidly as Bill, and, while he would proceed with the surgery, he was not optimistic of the outcome.

He recommended we participate in an experimental program where a medical device would be installed into Bill's abdomen with the hope that its release of time-controlled drugs would slow or stop the spread of the cancer.

We had difficulty obtaining the device, medication, and approval of the accompanying medical support team's coming to Memphis from Boston. The procedure was still mired in the Federal Drug Administration's bureaucracy.

Ole Miss law professor George Cochran, through a contact within the FDA, was helpful in expediting the required approval and assuring the experimental procedure could take place in Memphis.

The surgery took place in mid-March at Baptist Hospital on Madison Avenue in Memphis. It was long and unsuccessful. When the surgeon came to speak with me after the surgery, he said he had never seen a liver so completely encased with cancer.

Then he told me there was little hope for Bill to live.

From mid-March until early May, Bill was treated at Baptist Hospital.

That's where we were when Sydney Shaw, Ole Miss Chancellor Porter Fortune's executive assistant, called and asked if I would be interested in applying for the university attorney position. He asked if I could meet with Chancellor Fortune to discuss the position.

I replied that I could come from Memphis, but for only a short meeting, because I could not leave Bill for more than a few hours. We arranged a meeting time and date. I drove down I-55 to spend thirty minutes with the chancellor to discuss the position, ask what his expectations were, and when I should begin work if selected.

The only question I recall asking was if I could be free to attend the Browning Club meetings on Tuesday afternoons twice a month during the fall and spring.

"Mrs. Connell," Chancellor Fortune said, "if I did anything to interfere with the Browning Club, I could not go home. As you know, my wife, Lib, is a member of the club."

With that matter settled, I accepted the job, got back in my car, and rushed back to Memphis to be with Bill. I did not even ask what I would be paid.

During our two months of treatment in Memphis, Bill didn't respond. His situation quickly became grim.

Friends and family from Clarksdale and Oxford visited and sent many cards and letters. Bill was appreciative and moved by the show of affection and concern, especially the notes from people whose children he had photographed over the years. He repeatedly read a note from Polly Williams telling him how she and Parham treasured his pictures of their family.

In late April, the doctors told me there was nothing more they could do for Bill. He was hemorrhaging constantly and responding to nothing. They asked if I wanted them to stop all treatment, unplug the tubes, and allow nature to take its course.

I thought this was the right thing to do and agreed. Yet, I could not reach peace with the decision. As I stood looking out over Madison Avenue in Memphis, second-guessing myself, Martha and Dr. Joe Burnett, friends from Oxford, walked in the room where I was contemplating our options. Joe had recently had back surgery and was in the hospital there, too.

I talked through my dilemma with them. They could not provide an answer but told me to do what my heart and head thought was right. I then asked the doctors to reconnect the tubes with the desperate hope that a miracle would happen and something would work for Bill.

No miracle occurred.

Early in May, the doctors advised me to take Bill home. There was nothing more they could do for him.

I should have transported him home by ambulance, but I drove him myself. When we arrived at our home in Oxford, I could not lift him out of the car. I was in distress and did not know what to do, but then I thought of Duke and called his office. He was in trial, but he received permission from the judge to leave and come to our home, pick Bill up in his arms, carry him into the house, and put him in the bed.

For the next few weeks, Bill enjoyed the girls coming in and out until he eventually slept most of the time.

One day, Martha and Joe came by to visit. Bill fell asleep while we were talking.

"I know you must be having a difficult time financially," Joe said, "with the expenses of nursing care not covered by insurance. Let me know what you need, and I will loan it to you."

I did not have to call on him for the loan, but I will never forget his offer.

Bill died on May 25, 1982, at age fifty-five.

31

And in the streets the children screamed; the lovers cried, and the poets dreamed.
But not a word was spoken; the church bells all were broken.
And the three men I admire most; the Father, Son, and the Holy Ghost;
they caught the last train for the coast, the day the music died.

Don McLean, "American Pie"

The song was used to describe my husband, Bill, by Milly Moorhead in an editorial she wrote about him that was published on the front page of *The Oxford Eagle* on the day of his funeral. Bill had been a mentor to Milly and helped her learn to be a photographer because he believed in her talents. McLean's song was written about Buddy Holly, an American singer and songwriter, killed in his prime in a plane crash, and Milly's tribute to Bill was her way of memorializing him to the community of Oxford.

Bill's funeral was at St. Peter's Episcopal Church in Oxford. He was buried in the Connell family plot in Oakridge Cemetery in Clarksdale. Our friend, the Rev. Don Morse, returned from Trinity Church in Pass Christian, Mississippi, to officiate the funeral, along with the Rev. Doug Sterling, rector of St. Peter's.

As we lined up outside the church to proceed inside for the funeral, Natalie Richmond, a long-time Oxford friend, removed the flowers from the casket and placed the church's pall over his casket.

"You son-of-a-bitch," she muttered, "Why did you have to go and die on me? Now, who am I going to skip church with and go out to drink coffee and talk with during services?"

Jane, my nine-year-old daughter, asked me: "What is a son-of-a-bitch? Why is Mrs. Richmond calling Daddy a son-of-a-bitch?"

I explained that Mrs. Richmond loved her Daddy, would miss him, and these were her terms of endearment over her loss of her friend.

Cards, letters, flowers, contributions, and food poured in from Bill's legion of friends and family (Bill had been in twenty-seven weddings and had twenty-five godchildren). He valued relationships and never lost touch with a friend. He frequently received letters and calls from men with whom he had served in the Army in World War II and in the Air Force during the Korean conflict. He was a prodigious short note writer and stayed in touch with Culver Military Academy, military, fraternity, and Clarksdale friends through these notes.

With Bill gone, I had little money, four young daughters, and was mentally and emotionally lost. People deal with grief and loss in different ways. My way was to go back to work as quickly as I could and to tell the old stories that Bill told so well to keep his memory alive with the girls. Bill was a great storyteller and could always connect whatever story he was telling to the conversation of the moment. And, having lived in the Mississippi Delta most of his life, he had plenty of stories to tell.

One of the girls' favorite was about the time he and I were visiting various old friends in Clarksdale with Jane, our new baby. We went to see Suzy and Andy Carr, who had five children. Bill put Jane in her baby seat outside the Carrs' front door, rang the doorbell, and ran and hid with me in bushes out of sight of the door. Andy came to the door, looked down, and saw what appeared to be an abandoned baby at his front door, and began to call loudly and helplessly for Suzy.

"Someone has abandoned a baby at our front door! What are we going to do?"

At that moment, Bill stepped out laughing and saved the Carrs from a sixth child.

The girls and their friends also loved to hear the stories about the tricks Bill and A.C. Abraham played on each other. One year, A.C. entered Bill into the Mid-South Golden Gloves Boxing Competition in Memphis. Bill had been on the boxing team in boarding school at Culver Military Academy but had not boxed since that time. Bill received notice of his match right before Christmas.

Bill got even with A.C. by running an advertisement in *The Clarksdale Press-Register* on December 26.

Headline: **Wanted, Used Christmas Trees. Will Pay Premium Prices.**

The next line read: "Call A.C. Abraham for immediate pick-up and cash payment."

Bill's funeral was on a Thursday.

The following Monday, I entered the Lyceum, the main administration building for the University of Mississippi, to start my new job as university attorney at Ole Miss.

Bill, Christmas 1981

VII
University Attorney:
The Fortune Years

32

There are those rare times in life when people, places, and jobs are meant for one another. For me, the university attorney position at the University of Mississippi was just that — a symbiotic combination of all I could have hoped or dreamed.

I loved Ole Miss. I loved the law. I loved teaching. I loved supporting people who devote their lives to education.

If ever there were a perfect alliance — between a person and a job — it was at the moment Ole Miss Chancellor Porter Fortune selected me to succeed Tommy Ethridge as university attorney.

But my joy was overshadowed by Bill's death —and the daunting challenge of raising four daughters as a single parent.

Chancellor Fortune was understanding of my situation. He told me to take care of myself, come in when I could, spend as much time with Tommy Ethridge as possible, and know that the university family would be supportive and helpful to me during this difficult time in my life.

Tommy Ethridge, a fine lawyer and a true gentleman, took me around the campus and introduced me to the people who made the university run. Instead of sitting down and going over file after file and talking about the legal issues facing the university, Tommy advised me to be active on the campus, to get to know people, to go their offices for meetings, and to have a welcoming, open-office policy.

He also encouraged me to join — and be an active member of — the National Association of College and University Attorneys ("NACUA") organization. NACUA is the primary professional association serving approximately 4,000 attorneys who represent more than 1,400 campuses in the United States, Canada, and several other foreign countries. Tommy recommended that I get to know as many university attorneys around the country as possible. He also suggested I attend NACUA's annual conference.

Exactly one month after Bill's death, I traveled to New York City to attend the NACUA conference at the Waldorf Astoria Hotel. I took my daughters Stella, age thirteen, and Mary Ann, age twelve.

We checked in, and since I needed to get downstairs for the first official NACUA event, I taught Stella and Mary Ann how to order room service.

I took the elevator downstairs to the Waldorf's Grand Ballroom for the opening reception of the conference. I stepped into the ballroom. There were hundreds of university attorneys talking and laughing. Clearly, they knew each other. I felt very alone.

I don't know if I was still suffering the emotional trauma of losing Bill or the anxiety raising four daughters alone or simply dealing with the uncertainty of a new job, but I was miserable.

Standing still and lonely among this tight-knit group, I thought to myself, *I cannot do this. I want to go home.*

The last time I had felt this way was in 1949 at Camp Sequoya in Bristol, Virginia. I was eleven years old. I was the only camper from Mississippi. I was assigned to a cabin with five other campers and a college counselor.

The first camper I met, at the dining hall, asked me my name and where I was from.

"Mary Ann Strong," I answered, "from Louisville, Mississippi."

"You have two first names," she said, laughing at me, "and cannot even pronounce '*Louie*ville' correctly." Then she started to mock me, "And, just listen to your Southern accent."

I ran out of the dining hall, humiliated, back up the hill to my cabin. I fell down on my cot and cried. I wanted to go home. I was embarrassed and miserable and homesick.

I cried for about twenty minutes. Then I collected myself and walked back down the hill for evening vespers. I looked up at the stars and saw a constellation that had three stars in a straight line close together. I looked squarely at the middle star in the constellation of three and said to myself, "You are mine forever, and we are going to get through this together."

With my new star above me, I held up my head and said to myself, *Mary Ann, this is hard, but this is an opportunity. You can cry, beg to go home, make yourself and everyone around you miserable, miss a great experience in life... or you can hold your head up, put a smile on your face, walk back to the girl who humiliated you, and ask her what her name is and where she is from, enter into to the world around you, and make this night a turning point.*

That is exactly what I did. I deliberately sat next to the girl who mocked me. I asked her name (Nancy), where she was from (Pennsylvania), what family she had, what sports she liked, and how she chose to come to Camp Sequoya.

I realized no one at this camp cared that my parents were prominent in my small Mississippi hometown or that I was accomplished by the measuring rods used in Louisville, Mississippi. I understood, then, that I needed to toughen up and learn to think outside myself and be more interested in others.

I was reminded of a stanza in a poem:

Rebel, heretic, a thing to flout.
You drew a circle and shut me out.
But love and I had the wit to win.
We drew a circle and brought her in.

As I stood perfectly still in the middle of the Waldorf Astoria ballroom, tears welled up in my eyes. I wanted to flee back to my room.

The instant I remembered that moment from 1949, I noticed a man walk across the room and approach me.

"Mrs. Connell," he said, with a deep southern accent, "my name is Charlie Jacobs. I am from Cleveland, Mississippi. Our mutual friend, Kenneth Williams, told me you were coming and asked me to introduce you around."

Charlie, it turned out, was a member of the Board of Trustees of State Institutions of Higher Learning in Mississippi. He took my arm and introduced me to one nice person after another. I began to feel comfortable.

Within minutes, Mike Grier, Executive Director of NACUA, introduced himself to me in a genteel South Carolina accent. He welcomed me to NACUA and invited me to accompany him to meet other attorneys.

From that moment, I felt at home.

When I returned to our hotel room, I discovered that Stella and Mary Ann had mastered the concept of room service. They had ordered pizzas. Then, they placed a second order for ice-cream. And a *third* order of chips and Cokes.

When I returned to Oxford from the conference, I felt as if I had several thousand new law partners. I knew I could call on an attorney at any university over any matter and have instant help and guidance.

33

The first legal matter I handled for Ole Miss as university attorney was to serve as executor of the Estate of Dr. Victor Coulter. Dean Coulter had been dean of the College of Liberal Arts for many years and left the university the bulk of his estate. He named the university attorney as executor of his estate. His wife had predeceased him, and they had no children.

I had to assume dual roles of both lawyer and next of kin as I sorted through every material possession of Dr. Coulter's, paid his bills, and distributed his material possessions as he had directed, including renting a van and delivering several pieces of furniture to a relative in North Carolina.

He directed that his home on University Avenue be sold and the proceeds given to the university. We held a sale by sealed bid in the Board Room of the Lyceum. David and Debbie Bell were the successful bidders, and the house was deeded to them.

Shortly after handling Dean Coulter's estate, the University Museum inquired about obtaining the copyrights to some 350 paintings that artist Theora Hamblett had left the university.

Our patent attorney in Washington, D.C., was going to charge the university almost $30,000 to register the copyrights. I felt I could handle the matter for much less. I gave myself a lesson in how to obtain a copyright, and with the help of a friendly and competent contact at the Library of Congress, I went to Washington, D.C., and obtained the copyrights for the paintings. The cost to the university totaled $750 (my travel expenses).

Perhaps the most interesting legal dispute I handled in my first year as university attorney was an agreement made jointly by Alabama Coach Bear Bryant and Johnny Vaught.

In the 1970s, during Vaught's last year as athletics director at Ole Miss, the two men agreed they should put something in writing about the intent of each school to play the other for the next decade.

On the back of an envelope, they hand-wrote the following:

Ole Miss-Alabama

Home and away for ten years

$10,000 payment for no show

The envelope was signed:

Paul (Bear) Bryant

John Vaught

Alabama and Ole Miss played each other for four years after the agreement was executed by the two SEC legends. Ole Miss lost all four games by a combined 123 points.

In an effort to rebuild our football program — and with a new coach, Billy Brewer, coming on board — Ole Miss Athletics Director Warner Alford decided it might be a good idea to give our players a break from the Crimson Tide.

Warner notified the athletic administration at Alabama that we wouldn't be playing them for a few years. Alabama had no problem with the decision. They were immediately able to re-schedule another team to take our place.

Shortly thereafter, someone in the athletics administration at Ole Miss asked me to call Alabama's attorney to discuss payment of the $10,000 forfeiture fee based on the "envelope" contract.

I called an attorney I knew at the University of Alabama and explained to him why we needed to stop playing these games for a few years until we could get on stronger footing in football.

I told him that we would send our check for $10,000 immediately.

"Oh, no," he said, "You owe us $60,000 — $10,000 for each of the remaining years under the contract."

"We do not owe you $60,000." I replied. "We are not going to pay that amount, especially considering the vague wording on the back of the envelope."

"We will have to sue you for the $60,000," he responded.

"All right," I said, "you come on over to Oxford and sue us in the Circuit Court of Lafayette County, Mississippi."

I reminded him that the jury pool would be entirely from Lafayette County, that almost all of the potential jurors would have attended Ole Miss, worked at Ole Miss, or had children and other relatives who had done likewise.

"The jurors will be fair," I said. "I am sure of that. But you might want to think about whether you really want to walk into that courtroom as one of the nation's top teams, loaded with money, trying to get $60,000 from Ole Miss based on a 'contract' written on the back of an envelope, lacking the specificity required of a valid, binding agreement."

There was silence on the other end of the line.

After a moment, he said, "Well, forget what I said about suing you. Send the $10,000."

34

In the spring of 1982, the Ole Miss student body elected John Hawkins from Batesville, Mississippi, the school's first black cheerleader. During the summer leading up to football season, Hawkins said in an interview with *Gannett News Service* that he would not wave a Confederate flag at football games.

His statement, according to Professor David Sansing, "sparked a 'firestorm of protest' from Ole Miss traditionalists."

As the football season approached, rumors surfaced that the university would phase out the Confederate flag as the school's spirit symbol. The news evoked bitter anger toward Chancellor Fortune from both alumni and students. Many thought the administration had a secret scheme "to outlaw the flag," according to Professor Sansing.

At a press conference before the first football game in the fall of 1982, Hawkins explained why he would not carry a Confederate flag, as had been customary for male cheerleaders to do in the past.

"I am an Ole Miss cheerleader," he said "[which] makes me a representative of the whole student body — blacks and whites — but I am a black man, and the same way whites have been taught to wave the flag, I have been taught to have nothing to do with it."

The Ku Klux Klan quickly came to the aid of the flag. On October 21, 1982, a Thursday, Chancellor Fortune asked me to come to his office on the first floor of the Lyceum. He asked me to meet with a visitor to discuss a legal matter involving a possible demonstration on our campus by the Ku Klux Klan in support of the Confederate flag.

When I walked into the meeting, the chancellor introduced me to the grand wizard of the Ku Klux Klan for Mississippi and Louisiana.

He was dressed in a dark suit, white shirt, and tie. He did not have on a hood or robe. He explained that he was seeking permission to conduct a protest parade around the campus beginning in front of the Lyceum and marching around the Circle and Grove back to the steps of the Lyceum to raise the Confederate flag while the band played "Dixie."

Chancellor Fortune told the wizard that he did not want such a demonstration on the campus, but he would follow the law and rely on my legal advice as to whether, under the First Amendment, the university was compelled to permit the demonstration.

I told the chancellor and the wizard that I would need until the next morning to give a legal opinion. We agreed to reconvene at 9:00 a.m. Friday for my advice and opinion.

I immediately called Professor George Cochran. As he did every time I called on him for guidance and research, Professor Cochran came to my assistance. He guided me to the United States Supreme Court holding in *Healy v. James*, a 1972 case in which a college sought to ban a chapter of Students for a Democratic Society from campus.

I wrote Chancellor Fortune a memo on October 22, 1982, quoting what the *Healy v. James* Court wrote in deciding against the college:

> The mere disagreement of the President with the group's philosophy affords no reason to deny it recognition. As repugnant as these views may have been, the mere expression of them would not justify the denial of First Amendment rights. 408 U.S. 169, 283 (1972).

Quoting from a previous dissenting opinion of Justice Black in *Communist Party v. SACB*, 367 U.S. 1 (1961), the Court emphasized its position:

> I do not believe that it can be too often repeated that the freedoms of speech, press, petition, and assembly guaranteed by the First Amendment must be accorded to the ideas we hate or sooner or later they will be denied to the ideas we cherish. 408 U.S. 169 at 283, quoting *Communist Party*, 367 U.S. 1.

Several other cases, including one from the Fifth Circuit Court of Appeals, ruled the same way. In *Knights of the Ku Klux Klan v. East Baton Rouge Parish School Board*, 578 F.2d 1122 (5th Cir. 1978), a unit of the Louisiana Ku Klux Klan brought suit against a school board questioning the constitutionality of a policy under which groups advocating racial discrimination were excluded from use of school facilities. After finding that the school board in this case had historically permitted use of school facilities after hours by private organizations, the court held that prior restraint of the First Amendment rights of the Klan was clearly unconstitutional.

I knew Chancellor Fortune would be disappointed. I had no choice but to write him a memo explaining that as a public university with a limited public forum, we could not keep the Klan from demonstrating on our campus simply because we did not like their speech.

We could, however, regulate the time, place, and manner of the demonstration — but we could not prohibit it.

The next morning I returned to the chancellor's office, gave him my memo, and told the wizard that the university would give the Klan permission to demonstrate on the campus, but not in the areas he identified.

I proposed an alternate route for the demonstration: the back of the J.D. Williams Library and up to the building housing ROTC programs. The area was visible; the Klan's message could be seen and heard, and security could be provided.

The wizard did not like the alternate route and insisted that the Klan had a First Amendment right to demonstrate by the route they had originally identified.

"No," I said. "The route you propose will take you near the football field where we have 5,000 high school students from fully integrated schools participating in a band clinic; past the law school where the university is hosting a recruitment weekend for prospective minority law students from colleges and universities around the country; and past the Student Union Building where several black student organizations are holding meetings. In addition, a National Merit Scholars conference is being held along that route.

"That path presents a fear for the university of the possibility of fights and even a riot in light of the history of this institution."

The wizard, although remaining polite, kept arguing.

I told him that the university would seek a temporary restraining order to halt the demonstration on his desired path — and seek an immediate hearing before a federal judge to decide the issue.

With that, the wizard announced that the Klan no longer wanted to deal with the university. He said they would proceed with their demonstration around the town Square and on the streets of Oxford.

We parted ways.

The demonstration in Oxford did not draw the crowd that the Klan or the public had expected. The protest passed in a relatively calm manner. While thirty robed Klansmen marched up Jackson Avenue toward the Square, dressed in their white garb and hoods, waving Confederate flags, photographers from the Ole Miss annual staff took several photographs.

The Klan marched around the Square on October 23, 1982, and hoisted the Confederate flag in front of the Lafayette County Courthouse. All the while, a small band played "Dixie."

1982 Ku Klux Klan march in Oxford, MS
Photo by Robert Jordan

35

In 1983, Bill Battle picked me up in front of the Lyceum, the university's main administration building, in his maroon Lincoln town car.

"My office is in the trunk of my car," he said, as he put my travel items on the back seat.

His trunk was filled with licensing materials, samples of souvenirs, and other collegiate memorabilia.

Bill and I were traveling to the corporate offices of Russell Athletics in Alex City, Alabama, — one of the largest manufacturers and distributors of collegiate apparel in the world.

Ole Miss had worked with a patent and trademark attorney in Washington who handled the registration of seven of the university's marks — the Lyceum with red background and 1848, UMAA, Colonel Rebel, the Lyceum surrounded by "The University of Mississippi," the university's seal, "University of Mississippi," and "Ole Miss."

We produced a brochure explaining the licensing program we planned to initiate. The pamphlet was to be distributed to all persons interested in marketing any product bearing a registered University of Mississippi trademark.

As explained in the brochure, proceeds from our licensing program would be divided equally between the general fund and the athletics department, following deductions for administrative expenses.

Russell Athletics had historically been a consistent user of our newly-trademarked university symbols.

When Bill and I arrived at the offices of Russell Athletics, we were ushered into the conference room to meet with executives of the company and their attorney from Birmingham. The meeting was cordial until we explained that we expected Russell to enter into a licensing agreement with Collegiate Concepts, representing the University of Mississippi, by which

Russell would pay a licensing fee for use of any of the University of Mississippi's registered marks and logos.

The Birmingham attorney was competent, experienced, and gracious, but he was adamant that Russell had never paid royalties or licensing fees to use any university marks and logos and would not start doing so now.

We talked for quite a while about the legal cases around the United States in which courts had ordered companies using universities' copyrighted and registered marks to pay royalty fees or cease using the marks.

Even in the face of significant cases against his position, the Birmingham lawyer remained adamant.

As we were about to conclude the meeting and leave, I said to him: "You leave us no alternative but to sue you in federal court in Oxford, Mississippi, where you are doing business selling sporting apparel and memorabilia bearing registered and trademarked logos of the University of Mississippi without paying the university a licensing fee."

I continued, "You will enjoy spending time in Oxford. The town is lovely; the university is beautiful; and we will take you to see the home of William Faulkner and to nice restaurants and welcome you."

"We will, however, conclude your visit with a trip to the federal courthouse, where I think you will find that you will not prevail in your claim that you do not have to pay a royalty fee for use of these marks and logos protected under the United States patent and trademark registration process."

Two days later, Russell representatives contacted Bill Battle and me. They said they were ready to enter into a contract.

This was the beginning of the licensing program at the University of Mississippi. The contracts for this first year generated $38,000 in revenue for the university.

The 1983 Ole Miss yearbook was distributed to students in April. It provoked an angry response from black students.

The front pages of the annual featured major events of the school year, including several pictures of the robed Klansmen during the October rally. The subjects in the photograph were waving Confederate flags.

Initially, some of the black student leaders considered holding a book burning on the steps of the Lyceum. They eventually decided against this, but they refused to accept their annuals. And, they demanded a refund of their student activity fees allocated to the yearbook.

On Monday night, April 18, 1983, the night the rumored book burning was to take place, about 1,500 white students gathered at the Lyceum. Some waved Confederate flags; others were there curious to see what was going on.

Student government and fraternity leaders urged the students to go home, which most did. However, about 600 students marched to the Phi Beta Sigma house, John Hawkins' fraternity, and raised their Confederate flags, while shouting racial slurs and threats.

University and Oxford police eventually disbursed the crowd. Assistant Vice Chancellor Lucius Williams and Ardessa Minor, director of minority affairs, later reported that black and white students alike were unnerved by the demonstration at the Phi Beta Sigma house. They were troubled by how close the crowd was to becoming a mob.

Chancellor Fortune, who was at a meeting of the Southern Association of Colleges in Texas on the night of the demonstration, hurried back to the campus. At the urging of the faculty senate and other advisors, he decided to immediately make a public announcement regarding the Confederate flag. The address was originally scheduled for May.

Professor David Sansing and Willie Morris assisted Chancellor Fortune in writing his remarks. I walked from the Lyceum to the Turner Center auditorium on April 20, 1983, with Chancellor Fortune as he met the press and a packed audience.

He stood at the podium and said, "the Confederate flag never has been an official school symbol," and that "the University of Mississippi was officially and formally disassociating itself from the Confederate flag and that no unit or organization officially associated with the university, including cheerleaders, would display the flag."

He added that students not acting in an official capacity would be allowed to display the flag and the university's athletic teams, nicknamed the "Rebels," could continue using "Colonel Rebel" as their mascot. The band could also play "Dixie" as one of the school's official songs.

Chancellor Fortune added. "'Dixie' is outside my domain. It belongs to the public, and I do not propose to go around dictating who can play 'Dixie' and use the music or even who can whistle 'Dixie.'"

According to Professor Sansing, "That decision was one of the most unpleasant and difficult decisions of Chancellor Fortune's sixteen-year tenure. He was reviled by some of his long-standing friends and received several death threats. Others criticized Fortune for not disavowing 'Dixie' and Colonel Rebel."

Chancellor Fortune's action, courageous at the time, was the first act to change the image of the University of Mississippi, its culture, and its sensitivity to the feelings of others.

Chancellor Fortune announced that he would retire in 1984. The Board of Trustees of the State Institutions of Higher Learning (the IHL Board) conducted a national search for his successor.

While the search was proceeding, the university faculty circulated a petition endorsing the appointment of Governor William Winter, whose four-year term as governor was about to end. Impressed by this unusual show of unity, the board offered the position to Governor Winter.

He initially accepted the position, but upon further reflection declined it.

The board then resumed its national search.

The board favored a 38-year-old Texan.

On February 5, 1984, the IHL board announced its selection for the 14th Chancellorship of the university — and my new boss — R. Gerald Turner.

VIII
University Attorney:
The Turner Years

36

Chancellor Gerald Turner took the helm at Ole Miss when he was 38 years old.

He was the second-youngest chancellor in the university's history and among the youngest university presidents in the country.

The IHL board charged Dr. Turner with three primary goals: (i) increase enrollment, (ii) raise the image of the university nationally, and (iii) increase private funding.

Chancellor Turner hit the ground running. He was intelligent, full of energy, and committed to fulfilling the goals the IHL Board set for him.

Turner wasted no time setting the stage for his remarkable leadership. First, he appointed Robert Khayat as vice chancellor for university affairs. Next, he appointed Don Frugé as special assistant to the vice chancellor for university affairs. And shortly thereafter, he appointed Dr. Thomas Meredith as executive assistant to the chancellor.

Dr. Meredith had been serving at the IHL Board office. In fact, he had the primary responsibility for escorting Dr. Turner during the various interviews when he was in Mississippi during the search process.

Chancellor Turner's plan was simple: Khayat would be the university's external face; Frugé would build a credible private foundation to lead private financial support; Meredith would focus on day-to-day internal operations.

While this dream team was planning to meet the goals set out by the IHL, word had spread among the faculty and staff that the university had hired a female attorney. One of the first calls I received was from a woman in the accounting department.

"I'm so relieved we have a woman to turn to for legal help," she said.

"Thank you," I answered, "How may I help you?"

"I've got a lousy husband," she said, "and I need a quick divorce."

I gently explained that my job did not encompass obtaining divorces for university employees. She was disappointed. But not nearly as much as I was when I discovered that my duties did encompass another complicated, messy issue.

Two women, both of whom seemed anxious and agitated, came to see me. One woman worked at the receptionist's desk at the university's workout facility, the Turner Center. The other woman was her supervisor.

The receptionist had been enduring repeated, unwelcome touching, suggestions for after-hours meetings, and more from a professor who exercised at the center.

She was distressed, angry, and embarrassed.

"I like my job," she said. "I need my job."

She was afraid if she complained about the misconduct, she would be fired.

The alleged harasser was a professor of high standing within the university. I knew him well. We had children the same age. We attended the same church.

The woman and her supervisor turned to me for help.

That afternoon, I called the professor and told him I needed to come see him.

As I walked across campus, a fury grew inside me. I remembered feeling this way as a child when I threatened to shoot Stanley Hathorn in the eye. I walked into the professor's office and closed the door. I saw the color disappear from his face and his hands start to tremble. When I did not sit down, he knew why I was there.

"Don't you ever go into the Turner Center again," I said. "And do not ever do anything to hurt this young woman personally or professionally."

He nodded and looked down at the floor.

"If you do," I continued, "I will stand up in church and publicly accuse you of what you have done. And, before you say a word in response, if you want her to file formal charges and give you an opportunity to have a hearing before your peers on this accusation, you will be given that right."

There was a leaden moment of silence.

"I hear you," he said. "I will not go back. And I will not bother her or any other young woman again." Then he paused. "But please do not embarrass me by making any of this public."

I went back to my office, shut the door, and took a deep breath. Upon reflection, I knew there was a better way to handle the situation, but at the moment, it felt like the right thing to do.

It turned out I wasn't the only one cleaning up a mess created by others.

On Friday, July 18, 1984, Chancellor Turner called me to his office. He asked me to sit down as he picked up a stack of papers held together by a paper clip.

"Mary Ann," he said, "this is something no university president ever wants to receive."

He handed me the papers. It was an official inquiry letter from the NCAA. The letter announced the beginning of a formal investigation of allegations that the Ole Miss football team had violated NCAA rules.

As I flipped through the thirty-seven-page document, Chancellor Turner explained that the letter alleged forty-five rule violations. Following each allegation, there was a list of specific questions and requests for documents the enforcement staff wanted the university to provide.

Historically, the NCAA enforcement staff conducted investigations on their own with little involvement by the university in question. In our case, however, the NCAA staff asked Chancellor Turner if the university would like to be involved in a new, cooperative approach to the investigative process.

Chancellor Turner had so many questions about how to move forward. So did I.

37

Six months after he was hired — and two months after the NCAA letter of allegations — Chancellor Turner launched "The Campaign for Ole Miss." Its goal: raise $25 million.

"The major challenge with the campaign," Dr. Turner said, "would be convincing alumni that they should give to a public university."

The University of Texas at Austin had raised over $500 million in its campaign ending in 1983. Dr. Turner laminated an article about the campaign.

"If the richest state university has to raise private money to bolster their programs," he said to Ole Miss alumni, "what does that say for one of the poorest universities?"

A prominent alumnus, Frank Day, asked Chancellor Turner to visit his office in Jackson. Mr. Day told him to lower the announced goal of $25 million to $10 million.

"You are dooming your chancellorship by setting a goal that will fail," Day told him.

"We will not fail," Chancellor Turner replied. "We will exceed it."

Chancellor Turner, Robert Khayat, and Don Frugé traveled across the state and the nation, making hundreds of speeches to civic clubs, business organizations, alumni associations, and schools in an effort to enlist friends and alumni of Ole Miss, who had never before contributed to the university — or ever been asked to do so.

By the time Chancellor Turner arrived in 1984, the university had experienced three years of budget cuts from the state. There was no money for construction or maintenance.

Dr. Turner read an article in *The Chronicle of Higher Education* that stated that several universities were obtaining federal money to build research facilities. He went to visit with Will Hickman, a member of the Board of Trustees. Mr. Hickman was a close friend of Congressman Jamie Whitten, chair of the house appropriations committee. Dr. Turner asked Mr. Hickman what the university could do to help Congressman Whitten better understand the university's needs and goals.

Mr. Hickman advised the chancellor to visit with Congressman Whitten and invite him to campus for special events.

Shortly thereafter, the University of Mississippi hosted a "Jamie Whitten Day" and honored him in every way it could.

The gesture, we hoped, would give Congressman Whitten an opportunity to see first-hand the positive things the university was doing and to understand its goals and challenges.

38

As the NCAA awaited our response, Chancellor Turner and I had to answer the following questions:

- What should the university do in response to the NCAA requests?
- Should Ole Miss hire outside counsel or undertake the investigation internally?
- Should we engage in shared responsibility in this process?
- Were there institutional staff members capable of conducting an appropriate investigation, preparing a written response, and making an effective presentation before the NCAA Committee on Infractions should things come to that point?
- Were there institutional employees and/or representatives who had the time to devote to this labor-intensive investigation?

Chancellor Turner met with his executive team to determine how to respond.

The options were to hire outside legal counsel to defend the university at a cost that could range from $750,000 to $1,000,000. Another option was to conduct an internal investigation.

After much deliberation, Chancellor Turner agreed to participate in the NCAA's pilot program for internal investigation. He believed we had an institutional responsibility to run a clean athletics program with proper institutional control.

Chancellor Turner decided to appoint a team of university employees and alumni to respond to the allegations internally. I was included in that list. Our task: to work with the NCAA enforcement staff in a cooperative manner.

He appointed Dr. Tom Meredith, executive assistant to the chancellor, to chair the university's team. The rest of the team included Dr. Max Williams, professor of sociology, director of the Center for Population Studies, and chair of the Faculty Athletic Committee; Dr. Mickey Smith, former president of the Faculty Senate and chair of Health Care Administration; Emmett Marston, Esq., former president of the Alumni Association and partner in the Memphis law firm of Martin, Tate, Morrow, and Marston; Tom Mason, professor of law and associate dean of the School of Law; and me, the university attorney and a member of the university's athletic committee.

I inquired through NACUA (the National Association of College and University Attorneys) which other universities had recently undergone an NCAA investigation. Ted Mallo, attorney for the University of Dayton, told me that he had recently responded to an NCAA official inquiry. He offered to meet me in Washington, D.C., at the annual NACUA meeting and share with me his work product.

Ted's work proved to be invaluable in forming our investigation plan and formatting our response to the official inquiry.

Our team took the allegations and delved into them in an almost forensic manner. We assigned each member of the team responsibilities for investigating certain allegations. We traveled. We conducted interviews with student athletes, athletic boosters, and high school coaches.

Dr. Meredith and Mr. Marston took responsibility for allegations arising from recruitment issues in Arkansas and on the Mississippi Gulf Coast. Dr. Williams and I took responsibility for investigating allegations arising from recruitment issues in South Carolina; Louisiana; and Pascagoula, Mississippi.

We assumed the investigation would be time consuming, but we couldn't imagine its lasting impact.

In spite of the pending NCAA investigation, money started to flow into the university. Turner's "Campaign for Ole Miss" exceeded expectations and raised $61.7 million in cash gifts and deferred pledges during the official period of the campaign.

Our relationship with Jamie Whitten started to pay off, too. With the support of Mississippi's powerful congressional delegation – Whitten, Ole Miss alumni Thad Cochran and Trent Lott, and Senator John Stennis – millions of dollars were expended to establish or expand research centers at the university, including the Center for Computational Hydroscience and Engineering; the Center for Wetlands Resources; the Center for Wireless Communications; the Jamie Whitten Center for Physical Acoustics; the National Food Service Management Institute; and the Thad Cochran Center for the Development of Natural Products, the nation's only research facility devoted to the discovery and development of new pharmaceutical and agrochemicals derived from natural products.

In fact, Turner's fundraising team, led by Robert Khayat, was so prolific, in September 1986, Chancellor Turner initiated a "Drive for Athletics," to raise funds to expand the Oxford-University Baseball Stadium, the Starnes Athletic Training Center, and the Palmer-Salloum Tennis facility.

Archie Manning chaired the Drive for Athletics. He was the ideal person to lead this campaign. Again, Chancellor Turner, Khayat, and Frugé traveled extensively to speak to groups of alumni to emphasize the importance of private support for improving athletic facilities. They spent so many hours on the road eating at Wendy's, Don Frugé referred to the Wendy's drive-in as "the chancellor's dining hall."

The campaign raised $11.6 million.

The preliminary NCAA investigation dragged on for nearly two years.

Reports of the interviews and investigations were given to me. I wrote a response to each allegation for consideration by the team. All members of the team reviewed my response and made suggestions, which were incorporated into the final draft presented to Chancellor Turner for his approval.

Toward the end of that time, university representatives and members of the enforcement staff met at the Alumni House on campus to review more than sixty-seven allegations of wrongdoing. Through the cooperative approach, the university was able to share with the enforcement staff information we gathered — both in cooperation with them and on our own.

After the meeting, twenty-two of the sixty-seven were dismissed by the NCAA.

During the investigation, we often worked late into the evenings and sometimes early into the morning hours.

On one of those nights when we were down to the wire, I was in my office on the second floor of the Lyceum, with the door closed. It was very late. I was trying to finalize the report.

For most of the evening, I had been interrupted by team members with one question after another. As the hours wore on and the interruptions continued, I heard another knock on my door.

"Who is it!?" I quipped, irritated. "How in the world am I expected to get this written with these constant interruptions!?"

I heard a soft, courteous voice.

"This is Chancellor Turner and Dr. Meredith. May we come in for just a minute?" Embarrassed, I invited them in and apologized.

At this point, we all realized the toll this investigation had taken on us and on our families. We had *all* been away from our homes. I had missed my daughters' school plays and piano recitals. I missed spending time with my mother, who was undergoing cancer treatments.

The next day, we delivered the response of the university to the NCAA. A few weeks later, they responded to our report by dropping a number of the allegations.

We then submitted a rebuttal. In response to our rebuttal, several more allegations were dismissed.

Our internal investigation revealed possible violations of NCAA rules that required Chancellor Turner to declare some players ineligible in the upcoming Ole Miss-Tennessee game. The key players included J.R. Ambrose, the SEC's fifth leading receiver; starting offensive tackle Jay Shimmel; reserve defensive backs Derrick Lindsey and A.D. Matthews; and Lester Brinkley, defensive tackle.

On November 14, 1986, after a ninety-minute conference call with the NCAA in which Dr. Max Williams and I presented the case to reinstate the players for the Tennessee game, the NCAA ruled for Ole Miss.

Athletics Director Warner Alford kindly credited me, in part, with the reinstatement of the players. "Dr. Connell has been heading all this up from the beginning," he said. "Her presentation of the facts and the way she outlined it had as much to do with the ruling as anything."

The reinstated players were allowed to play in the Ole Miss-Tennessee game the next day. Ole Miss lost 22-10.

The next day, following the Ole Miss-Tennessee game, a contingency of university representatives flew to Kansas City for a formal hearing before the Committee on Infractions, which lasted over twelve hours.

I thought we presented our case well. The Committee on Infractions was complimentary of the chancellor and our team. But we knew we would receive sanctions.

The university was placed on probation for a two-year period and prohibited from participating in any post-season competition following the 1987 football season. The team was also prohibited from appearing on any telecast involving live coverage during the 1987 season.

In addition, no more than twenty new recruits in football (rather than the normal limit of thirty) would be permitted to receive initial grants-in-aid at the institution during the 1987-88 academic year.

Because ethical conduct citations had been issued against two of our assistant coaches by the Committee on Infractions, the university informed them by letter from Chancellor Turner on December 7, 1986, that their contracts would not be renewed.

These sanctions caused a significant loss of income from television and bowl game revenues.

It also caused the university great embarrassment.

Even greater, however, was the emotional cost to the university family. So many of us had been students together at Ole Miss. In fact, many of my college friends fell on opposite sides of the issues. There were many different opinions about how the situation should have been handled. Some alumni thought the investigative team was too hard on our athletic representatives and did not fight hard enough to vindicate their actions.

Others thought it was mistake to have me — a woman — take a leadership role in a matter about athletics.

Some blamed Chancellor Turner for not being supportive enough of the Ole Miss coaches and players even in the face of overwhelming evidence of their violating NCAA rules.

But Chancellor Turner also received letters of appreciation from many alumni thanking him for his leadership in this matter.

I also received letters of support.

Perhaps the most touching correspondence came from Ole Miss player J.R. Ambrose. He mailed me a card. It had a simple, two-word message: "Thank you."

39

The NCAA investigation took its toll on me in many ways. But my biggest regret, undoubtedly, was the time I missed with my mother.

As a young woman in Louisville, my mother had been a well-respected teacher. She was strict and demanding, but also helpful and beloved by her students.

This was in the midst of the Great Depression. My mother's money was deposited in a bank that failed. My father, who represented the bank, offered to pay my mother ten cents on the dollar for what she had deposited.

At the time he made the offer, they were on a date at a picnic at a nearby lake. My mother was enraged at him over the offer and told him so.

My father reacted just as angrily. After a heated exchange, he pushed her into the lake. She emerged soaking wet.

"You," she said, "are going to have to pay for me to go to the beauty shop to fix my hair."

My father agreed.

He paid for weekly beauty shop appointments for the next thirty years.

My mother and my father began dating regularly after the lake incident, much to the consternation of the school principal and superintendent.

The two men called my mother in and told her that Bill Strong was a "ladies' man." They said he was known, on occasion, to drink alcohol and play cards — all of which made him unacceptable as a suitor for one of their teachers.

Even though she was one of the school district's most respected teachers, they gave her an ultimatum: "Stop seeing Bill Strong, or you will be fired."

"That will not be a problem," my mother told them. "We will not be dating anymore. We are going to be married the day after this school semester ends, and I will be resigning my position."

When I think about my parents, I remember their absolute devotion to one another. There was a magic in their relationship that brought joy to my life.

Our family lived an unusual lifestyle for the time. My parents did not get up early in the morning. We never had breakfast together. And we never sat down at 6:00 p.m. for dinner as most of my friends' families did.

Instead, my father would return from his office about 5:30 p.m., and he and my mother would sit under a pecan tree in our yard and have cocktails together. I would generally eat cereal or whatever was left over from lunch and be on my way to the myriad of activities I was involved in at the time.

My parents frequently cooked after I left and had dinner together without me. I never thought it was unusual.

My mother was an outgoing, warm, and loving person. She was always welcoming to my friends and was genuinely interested in their lives. She loved to have them in our home, and they loved to come there because she was so gracious. I have tried to demonstrate the same interest in my children's friends and have hosted dozens of parties for them. When Mary Ann graduated from Oxford High School, I hosted a party for the senior class and served my specialty, chicken tetrazzini (fancy name for chicken spaghetti). Warren Wells asked me for more lemonade. I reached into the refrigerator, took out a pitcher of a clear, lemony-looking liquid and filled his glass. He took one sip and nearly choked. I had served him chicken broth instead of lemonade.

Mother was fully engaged in activities of the Methodist Church and my activities at school. She was active in the Fortnightly Club, a ladies' literary club that met twice a month in the home of its members, and she loved to play bridge. She was patient with me as she tried to teach me to be a good bridge player, but I did not have the natural card sense she had — likely due to her skills in math that I did not inherit.

My daughters adored "Mimi." Truly loved her. Mimi did not shower them with gifts, but she attended all their school events and bought them clothes for special occasions. She spent much time in my home as her health failed. My daughter Mary Ann was a senior in high school during her last year and was especially kind and sweet to Mimi. She would take her back to her apartment at the end of every day and sing songs with her as they rode.

My mother died in my home on March 7, 1987.

Her funeral was held in the Oxford-University United Methodist Church. The Reverend Larry Goodpaster conducted the service and preached a meaningful sermon extolling the character of her abundant life. He said he would always recall watching her on the fourth row, left side, of the church as he preached his Sunday sermons to see her facial reactions. One day when he thought he was preaching an unusually good sermon, he saw her raising her left arm and pointing to her watch. He knew that was her signal to him that it was nearing noon and time to cut the sermon off so that she could return to her apartment to view the kickoffs of the professional football games.

After the service in Oxford, we traveled back to Louisville where Mother was to be interred in the family plot in the cemetery there between my father and brother. It was pouring down rain. As we approached the site, I burst into tears as I saw 50-60 old family friends huddled together under a tent awaiting our arrival to pay their last respects to a woman they loved deeply. After the graveside service, Jen and Davis Fair hosted a reception in their home on East Main Street for all who were in attendance. That gave my children and me an opportunity to express our appreciation to those old friends who had enriched my mother's life and mine.

In many ways, I was a good daughter. I held luncheons for my mother and introduced her to all my friends. I even attended the Methodist Church with her because it meant so much to her to have me and her grandchildren with her.

But I have deep regrets for the things I did not do. I did not take her to visit friends and family in Alabama. I did not really listen to her when she needed to talk. I neglected to ask her questions about her childhood or demonstrate interest in details of her life that she would have loved to talk with me about.

I was self-centered. Too wrapped up in my own life and work. Too consumed with trying to fill the void that I'd carried since my brother's death by obtaining accolades and honors.

I sometimes demonstrated disapproval of the way my mother did things when they were not exactly to my liking. I did what I should have done in many ways, but not with the warmth and caring that I wish that I had given.

She and my father, and their beautiful relationship with each other, made me into the woman I am. I regret that I did not tell them more often how much I loved, admired, and appreciated how special they were to me.

I expressed those feelings in dozens of letters I'd written while at summer camp, at Ole Miss, at Rena Lara, and in Oxford, but I did not express those feelings face to face.

It would have meant far more to them. And to me had I done so.

40

On March 26, 1987, while still dealing with the loss of my mother, I was on the phone with an attorney from Jackson. In the middle of the conversation, Margaret Sims walked into my office to interrupt.

"You need to get off the phone. Something terrible has happened."

Earlier that day, twenty-five members of the Chi Omega sorority participated in a twenty-five mile walkathon from Batesville, Mississippi, to Oxford to raise money for the Mississippi Kidney Foundation.

The walk took place along Highway 6.

In previous walkathons, the Mississippi Highway Patrol had provided cars, one in front of the walking girls and one in the back with blue lights flashing. This year, the Highway Patrol told the sorority that they could not provide the protection offered in the past. They advised the girls to stay off the highway and stay on the shoulder. The girls took matters into their own hands. They designated a lead car with hazard lights flashing and a trailing car, driven by Margaret Gardener, with hazard lights flashing.

It was a beautiful, spring Mississippi day. Fannie and Bee Elliott of Oxford were driving to Jackson that morning and passed the girls starting their walk in Batesville. They waved to them. One was their daughter, Maggie.

The girls had covered about fifteen miles of the trek on the shoulder of Highway 6 when a one-ton truck towing a hay baler topped a hill and came upon the group. The driver tried to veer away, but the truck slammed into the rear of the trailing car. The impact propelled the car, the truck, and the hay-baler into the girls.

Five of the girls were killed: Margaret Emily Gardner, Mary Pat Langford, Elizabeth Gage Roberson, Robin Renee Simmons, and Ruth Hess Worsham. Eleven others were injured. Maggie Elliott's pelvis was broken in four places, and one of her legs was crushed. Another girl's leg was amputated above the knee.

Chancellor Turner made arrangements for and held a memorial service for the injured and deceased young women in Tad Smith Coliseum the following day.

It usually takes days, even weeks, to set the coliseum up for such an event, but under the chancellor's direction, and that of Patricia Huggins and Leone King, the arrangements were accomplished overnight. Over 3,000 attended the memorial service the following day.

Before the memorial service, Chancellor Turner whispered, "This is the worst day of our lives."

I could only imagine the loss those families and friends were experiencing.

One of the girls who was killed, Beth Roberson, was enrolled in the business law class I taught on Monday evenings.

The first class meeting after the accident, a hush fell over our classroom. As I checked the roll, the students in the class stared at the empty seat on the second row.

The seat Beth had occupied.

41

In late November of 1987, Paul Kurta, co-producer with Heartbreak Productions, a Los Angeles film company, asked Chancellor Turner for permission to film a portion of a movie on the Ole Miss campus. The working title was *Heartbreak Hotel*.

Dr. Turner asked Dr. Meredith and me to take the lead in working with the film company and negotiating a contract for filming. The shoot would take place during April and May 1988.

Dr. Meredith and I met with Peggy Coleman, a production manager, to discuss what the company needed and what it would expect of the university.

Ms. Coleman was resistant. She didn't want to address practical matters until the chancellor had given permission to use the campus.

"We're going to be running in circles," I told her, "unless we address practical concerns first."

I explained that any one of them could become an item that would preclude further discussions. The items I wanted to address seemed reasonable — location and use fee; use of sorority and fraternity names and houses; dates of filming; lock-down of portions of the campus; blocking off of streets; locating alternative parking for film company vehicles; and non-use of identifiable university names and logos.

Instead of discussing and working through these details, Heartbreak Productions sent us a location agreement.

I found the agreement unacceptable and rejected it on behalf of the university.

The film company then asked for more meetings, but they continued to resist giving us details about their needs and expectations until the chancellor gave permission to film the movie on campus.

I reiterated that the chancellor was not going to give permission until he was satisfied that we had achieved a definite understanding of what responsibilities the university would incur and what benefits it would receive from the association.

Reluctantly, the film company began to answer our questions.

They needed a "lock up" or cordoning off of several areas so they would have control over the entrance to the campus, from the chemistry building to the Johnson Commons, for two days of shooting.

One of those days would be filming the scene where the star, Ally Sheedy, arrives on campus and drives around the Lyceum area.

The other day would be a "walk-talk" scene in front of the Lyceum.

They would also need a lock up of an area of the campus around an academic building where interior shots of classrooms and professors' offices would take place. The company anticipated ten days for preparation work, such as painting and placing of signs to reflect "Randolf University," and filming.

The university would have to provide parking spaces for four large fifty-foot trucks, five smaller trucks, four thirty-five-foot mobile motor homes for the stars, a camera crane, several maxi vans for the crews, and parking spaces for twenty-five crew members in portions of the campus near the filming site.

They would bring their own caterers and kitchen on one of the trucks, but the university would need to provide facilities for their dining.

The film company wanted to arrive on campus and begin work on February 29, 1988, and complete work by June 15, 1988.

We informed them that there were certain time periods when the campus could not be locked down and filming could not go on, such as during the Red-Blue game, Dixie Week, final exams, commencement, and the beginning of summer school.

Dr. Meredith and I met again with representatives of the company and their Los Angeles lawyers to attempt to finalize terms of the agreement.

The film company proposed a use fee of $250.00 a day.

At that point, I closed my file, stood up, and told them that we did not need to talk any more.

Kurta asked if we had considered a minimum fee.

"Our use fees," I told him, "will be tied directly to what areas of the campus you will be using and to our responsibilities." I added, "It will not be worth our time to be involved for even a day for under $15,000."

He seemed stunned by the amount, but I was adamant.

"We will see what we can do," he said.

After many more meetings, the details were worked out. We agreed to have removable letters "Randolf University" placed on the woodwork above the columns of the Lyceum, as well as on an archway over the street near Ventress Hall. We also agreed to remove vending machines, no smoking signs, and bulletin boards from the Old Chemistry building. And we agreed upon colors to paint the interior of a classroom in Old Chemistry.

I prepared a letter of agreement for Chancellor Turner's signature dated February 29, 1988, setting forth terms of the agreement reached in our discussions.

The agreement was long and detailed, specifying what areas of the university could be used for filming or production (the Lyceum exterior, circle in front of Lyceum, Harrison Room in the library, auditorium in Old Chemistry, infirmary, and exterior of sorority row), with a fee of $15,000 and $1,500 for each additional shooting day thereafter.

We included usual requirements of certification of insurance, indemnification of the university, and requirements regarding the care of the premises.

Production began. The name of the movie was changed to *Heart of Dixie*.

The filming was a major disruption to campus life. The producers constantly changed location requests. Each time, we had to remove all cars from sorority row, relocate classes in the Old Chemistry building when filming was going on in adjoining classrooms, or block off entire sections of campus.

When the project was completed, Peggy Coleman, the production manager, wrote the physical plant staff a letter "expressing a million thanks on behalf of the whole cast and crew for all your co-operation and assistance during filming."

Heart of Dixie starred Virginia Madsen, Phoebe Cates, and Treat Williams in addition to Ally Sheedy. It opened August 25, 1989, and grossed a grand total of $1,097,333 at the box office.

42

To address the second of his three major charges from the IHL board, Chancellor Turner initiated an aggressive student recruitment program. Under his leadership, and with strong assistance from Meredith and Khayat, colorful recruitment brochures were distributed throughout the nation. Student recruiters were sent out across Mississippi and the South to tout the advantages of Ole Miss.

A primary focus of the recruitment effort was attracting African-American students. During his first few months in office, Chancellor Turner spoke and preached in African American churches. He announced that any African American student admissible to graduate school would be given a tuition waiver and a $2,200 stipend.

Chancellor Turner was committed to making Ole Miss more welcoming to black students. As part of his commitment to diversity, Dr. Turner appointed Dr. Donald Cole, an African-American male, as associate dean of the graduate school and associate professor of mathematics, and Mary Thompson as a senior staff member in the financial aid office. He appointed Mike Edmonds as assistant dean of students,

Mike Edmonds suggested to Chancellor Turner that he should establish an awards program to honor the heroes of Mississippi's civil rights movement and to recognize a new generation of black leaders.

Turner welcomed Edmonds' proposal and established the first Awards of Distinction, an annual ceremony that gives special recognition to a select group of black Mississippians.

The first Award of Distinction was given to Reuben Anderson, the first black graduate of the law school and the first black justice of the Mississippi Supreme Court.

Chancellor Turner's goals to enhance the university's public image — the most difficult of the challenges the IHL board had given him — seemed insurmountable.

While Chancellor Turner was trying to minimize, if not limit, the public display of the Confederate flag at university events, the editor of the *Daily Mississippian*, the student newspaper, wrote that "'heaven… is full of Rebel flags.'"

In August 1988, the Eta Beta Chapter of Phi Beta Sigma, an African American fraternity, was preparing to move into a house on all-white fraternity row.

Chancellor Turner took an active role in integrating the houses by working with alumni and the national office of Phi Beta Sigma. He worked with local banks to encourage financing of the house. Chancellor Turner said he saw it as a way to send a signal "that the movement toward equality was continuing."

The house was spruced up over the summer and was ready for Phi Beta Sigma to move in.

Instead, on the morning of August 4, 1988, the empty house exploded in flames.

Fire investigators found a can of paint thinner in a second-story closet. The state officially labeled the fire arson.

Chancellor Turner was furious.

Sparky Reardon, associate dean of students; Thomas Wallace; and Stuart Brunson, president of the Interfraternity Council, solicited help from other Greek organizations on campus and the community. Governor Ray Mabus was one of the first to contribute to the fund.

An Ole Miss alumnus, who asked to remain anonymous, offered to underwrite a $100,000 mortgage to build a new house for the fraternity. The university offered a $6,000 reward for the arrest and prosecution of the arsonist.

The team raised enough funds for the Phi Beta Sigmas to purchase and furnish another house on Fraternity Row.

But Fraternity Row wasn't through with its racist acts.

On September 18, 1989, a Beta Theta Pi fraternity member and a pledge were stripped naked, blindfolded, and driven twenty-seven miles north to Rust College, a small, predominantly black, private school in Holly Springs, Mississippi. Their hands and feet were bound with duct tape and their naked bodies painted with "KKK" and a racial slur, "We hate niggers."

The students, who were white, were removed from the vehicle in which they had been transported and left abandoned on the campus at 1:00 a.m.

Rust College security officers contacted the Ole Miss police department. University police officers retrieved the students and returned them to Ole Miss.

Chancellor Turner expressed anger and shock over the incident. "Unquestionably," Turner told the *New York Times*, "this action of a few has reflected very negatively on the university community in such a way as to deny the significant advancements in human relations that have occurred on campus in the past few years."

Chancellor Turner immediately called the president of Rust College to apologize. Then, he dispatched the president and treasurer of the fraternity, who was also president of the Interfraternity Council, to Holly Springs to apologize to officials there.

Six days later the president of the Interfraternity Council resigned his position and apologized, saying, "I'm deeply sorry to the university."

Beta Theta Pi representatives said this was a fraternity prank that got out of hand.

Chancellor Turner appointed a discipline committee of four faculty and staff members and one student and, after a hearing, expelled one student and suspended four others. All of the five students involved were from out of state.

The chancellor banned Beta Theta Pi from the university for three years and ordered the fraternity to close its house on fraternity row.

As Professor David Sansing pointed out, these two events, the burning of the Phi Beta Sigma house and the Beta incident, were negative reflections of Ole Miss, but many positive events were simultaneously taking place. The Ole Miss fraternity system was being slowly integrated as Damien Evans, a black student and son of Coach Rob Evans, joined Sigma Chi Fraternity;

Kappa Alpha Psi, a black fraternity, inducted two white students; and Carl Lee Powell was elected ASB treasurer the following spring. Kimsey O'Neal, a black pharmacy major and an academic all-American in basketball, was elected Miss Ole Miss.

The student body also elected Chucky Mullins Colonel Rebel, the second black student to receive that honor. During the Ole Miss-Vanderbilt game on October 29, 1989, Mullins suffered a severe spinal injury. Ole Miss fans and friends raised more than $1 million to help him deal with the debilitating paralysis.

The Phi Beta Sigmas established the Chucky Mullins Courage Award, which is given each year to a senior defensive back who displays the courage and heart that characterized the life of Chucky Mullins. The recipient of the award each year wears Chucky's jersey number, 38.

In spite of these positive events — and the chancellor's commitment to change the image of the university — when it came to public perception, Ole Miss was stuck in "one step forward and two steps backward."

43

My brother, Billy's, death had been the dominating event of my life. I thought about it every day. I imagined what Billy would have been like if he'd had the opportunity to grow older.

I vicariously had him go to college, marry, have children, and become a smart, loving man. Those daydreams remained a part of my daily life for nearly fifty years.

Then, one day I looked across the room during an administrative council meeting. I realized I did not have to live in a make-believe world anymore.

I was looking at a man — Gerald Turner — who looked very much like what Billy would have looked like. He had the qualities I knew Billy would have had — intelligence, kindness, and compassion.

That prescient moment gave me a sense of inner peace.

As I walked out of the office that day and into the hall of the Lyceum, I met Dr. Vaughan Grisham walking in.

I had known and respected Dr. Grisham for years. He was a fine professor. We chatted for a few minutes.

"I don't think you remember this," he said, "but I am the little boy down the street on South Columbus Avenue in Louisville who played with Billy."

Tears filled my eyes. Tears of sadness. And tears of joy that someone else still remembered Billy.

One afternoon in 1989, Chancellor Turner called me into his office. "Mary Ann," he said, "you've done outstanding work."

"Thank you," I answered. "It's my dream job."

"You need to take some time away from the university," he said. "Do something different."

I thought for a moment he might be firing me.

Chancellor Turner said he wanted to recommend to the university's governing board, the IHL Board, that I be given a professional leave with half salary for a year — a leave comparable to a sabbatical for a faculty member.

He thought since I had raised four daughters as a single parent (having been widowed at forty-four), I needed a break from university work.

I was overwhelmed with appreciation and responded that I would explore job opportunities at other universities, in Washington, or a temporary position with a law firm with an education law practice.

A few days later, Chancellor Turner called me back into his office.

"You are a student at heart," he said. "You should take this opportunity and go back to school."

He assured me he would give me the best recommendation, as long as I started at the top in my efforts to be accepted into an LL.M. program at a major American university.

I immediately applied to the law schools I thought were the best in the United States: Harvard, Yale, Stanford, Texas, Virginia, Chicago, and Michigan.

A few weeks after the conversation with Chancellor Turner, I attended the annual conference of the National Association of College and University Attorneys in Boston. While there, I scheduled a meeting with the director of the graduate program at the Harvard Law School, Athena Mutua.

On the day of our meeting, I took a cab from the Marriott at Copley Place to the ILS Building at the Harvard Law School. I arrived early and walked around Harvard Yard, the area around the law school, and the town of Cambridge. I was so nervous I could hardly make myself go in for the meeting.

Athena was warm and welcoming.

"If you are awarded a degree from Harvard Law School," she said, "many doors will open for you. So… let me ask you why you want to enter Harvard's graduate law program."

I responded that I wanted to learn, to broaden my horizons, and then return to Oxford, Mississippi, as a better lawyer and teacher.

I told Athena that I was like William Faulkner when he visited his friend Sherwood Anderson in New Orleans in his early writing years. After repeated rejection by major publishing companies, Faulkner reportedly said to Anderson, "I just can't write anything that anyone wants to read."

"Go home, Bill," Anderson responded, "to your native soil, and write about the people and places you know and love." And that is what Faulkner did.

As he put it, "I returned home to Oxford, Mississippi, to that little two-cent postage stamp of earth that was mine and began to write."

"That," I explained to Athena, "is what I want to do. I want to go home to my little postage stamp of earth with my Harvard education and do my best to make my part of the world a better place."

While I daydreamed about attending law school for an advanced degree at places far beyond my reach, I was regularly reminded of exactly where I stood.

Student disciplinary matters abound on college campuses. Many lawyers do not understand that a university has the right and responsibility to address such matters on the campus, no matter what may be going on in the civil or criminal world. On many occasions through the years, attorneys, especially from Jackson, called threatening to sue the university if we did not drop discipline charges against their clients for public drunkenness, disorderly conduct, or such.

They generally maintained that such charges constituted double jeopardy if their client was also being tried in Oxford City Court or the Circuit Court of Lafayette County.

They were mistaken.

The university has no authority to incarcerate or fine a student. However, it does have the authority to take appropriate disciplinary action for violation of university rules. A university is a different forum, and its actions do not constitute double jeopardy.

One day, a friend and former college peer called me. He was furious. His son had been arrested. The charges: public drunkenness, disturbing the peace, indecent exposure, resisting arrest, and failing to respond to commands of a law enforcement officer.

"My son has never had a drink of alcohol," he exclaimed.

I told my former classmate that I would look into the matter.

I returned his call after speaking to the arresting officers and delivered the news.

"Your son was arrested at 1:00 am after the home game against LSU for attempting to direct traffic at an intersection in Oxford known as 'Panic Junction' while drunk…and naked."

My college friend got very quiet.

"Just disregard what I said about suing the university," he said. "It looks as though my problem is with my son."

44

The first response I received from the applications I had submitted was from Harvard.

I was so nervous, my hands shook as I opened the letter. I was so filled with emotion that I did not trust my own judgment. I wasn't sure what the letter said.

I asked Margaret Sims, my assistant, to come read the letter and tell me what it said.

Margaret held the letter in her hands, looked up at me, and smiled.

"You got in."

I began the process of finding a place to live in Cambridge or Boston and arranging for someone to cover my duties at the university and someone to take care of my home.

Chad Lamar, a young man from Oxford, had been living at 504 Beacon Street in Boston for the past year, getting his LL.M. at Boston University.

Chad's mother, Pat Lamar, had exquisite taste and had furnished the apartment. I took over the remaining year of Chad's lease. In return, Pat agreed to leave the apartment furnished, and I was to arrange to have the furnishings returned to Mississippi at the end of my year there.

The apartment, on the fourth floor of an old building at the corner of Massachusetts Avenue and Beacon Street, was lovely. There was a large living room with a fireplace overlooking Beacon Street, a small kitchen and breakfast area, and a long hallway back to a large master bedroom with a fireplace overlooking the Charles River. In the bedroom, there were two wrought iron beds and a desk in front of the window looking over the Charles, where I spent hours both working at my computer and watching the crew teams practice. Best of all, there was a parking place immediately back of the building reserved for apartment 504. An additional perk was the bus stop for bus #1 that went from Boston to Cambridge Square was right outside my front door. I could not have had a better living arrangement.

Before I left Oxford for the trip to Cambridge, E. Grady gave me Robert Bork's book, *The Tempting of America*, with a personal message inscribed: "For dear Mary Ann as an immunization shot for all that you will hear next year. Grady, Aug. 11, 1990."

While our love and admiration for each other had not changed through the years, our political and philosophical views of the role of government had taken different paths as we had grown older.

Studying in the Harvard Law Library, circa 1991

45

In September 1990, I walked down the aisle at the opening convocation of Harvard Law School.

I followed a 173-year-old tradition. I entered my name, date and place of birth, and my parents' names into the great enrollment book:

Mary Ann Strong Connell, October 12, 1937, Louisville, Mississippi; parents, William Augustus Strong, Jr. and Mary Emma Danzey Strong; date and place of birth, Louisville, Winston County, Mississippi.

It was not only a powerful moment for me, but also a moment of disbelief. How could I be in this place signing my name in a book that had welcomed Oliver Wendell Holmes, Jr., Felix Frankfurter, William J. Brennan, Learned Hand, Henry Cabot Lodge, Louis Brandeis, Richard Posner, Anthony Kennedy, John Roberts, Antonin Scalia, Roscoe Pound, Barney Frank, Henry Blackmun, Loretta Lynch, and Kathleen Sullivan?

I assumed everyone here was probably smarter than I, tested higher on all the standardized tests, attended more prestigious educational institutions, and lived and moved in New England social and intellectual circles unfamiliar to me. How did I, at age fifty-three, growing up in a small town in a small state in the Deep South, arrive at this place?

I longed for my parents. I wanted my teachers from Louisville, Mississippi, and from the University of Mississippi to be with me. They had all played a part in making this moment possible. But one person, more than all others, gave me this opportunity – Chancellor Gerald Turner.

My first day of class, I was up early. I wore a conservative dress, heels, and stockings, and carried a purse. I caught bus #1 across the Charles River, passed MIT, and arrived at the Law School.

I walked into Room 101 of Pound Hall, a large room with seats in a semicircular rise. I was terrified. All of a sudden, there I was, alone, with 110 members of my LL.M. class.

The students were from all over the world. They were half my age and looked like my children. They wore jeans, carried backpacks, all seemed to know each other, and appeared to be self-assured about everything.

I was fifty-three years old, dressed for work, and looked and felt out of place. I took a seat on the second row next to a young man with a warm smile. He introduced himself.

"I am Terry," he said. "I'm from Hong Kong."

From that moment on, he became "Mr. Harvard" to me.

Orientation began with Athena Mutua's giving one of the most inspiring talks I have ever heard on living an abundant life while at Harvard. She had been in the LL.M. program herself a few years earlier and spoke to us from that perspective. She encouraged us to reach out and make the most out of this experience. With a smile that enveloped the whole room and an enthusiasm that made even the most sophisticated student want to jump up and shout, she said, "Reach out and savor every minute of this day and the remaining days of your year here. Get to know each other. Learn about each other's cultures, families, and backgrounds. Go to hear every speaker you can. Open your mind and your heart to all that you are exposed to, and be the best that you can be."

Knute Rockne could not have done it better. I was so excited and fired up by this point that all my fears and reservations were forgotten.

During the first break of the morning session, I introduced myself to ten or more of my classmates and found that underneath their seemingly urbane, composed exteriors, they were just as unsure of themselves and intimidated as I.

I asked several students to join me for lunch. We wandered about Harvard Square until we selected a salad restaurant where we began our first of many shared meals in Cambridge together.

Harvard's LL.M. program had a number of specialized areas, such as taxation, corporate finance, and international corporate transactions. It also had something particularly attractive to me – a general LL.M. where a student could craft his or her courses to fit his or her special area of interest. For me, it was education law. The only required course in this general LL.M. field was theories of law, a philosophy course. My schedule for the year included constitutional law, employment law, disability law, race and American law, higher education law, and sexual orientation and the law.

Professor Randy Kennedy taught the race, racism, and American law classes. We spent a great deal of time discussing employment discrimination law, and the shifting burden of proof.

During one of the lectures, I was hopelessly lost. I knew this topic — the burden of proof — would revisit us on the final examination. Being older than most of my classmates and having a pronounced Southern accent, I was reluctant to raise my hand and ask Professor Kennedy to review the topic again.

At this moment, the handsome, well-respected editor of the *Harvard Law Review*, who was sitting to my right on the row behind me, raised his hand and said: "Professor Kennedy, please go back over this subject once again. I am not sure that I understand it."

The professor smiled.

"All right, Mr. Obama," he said, "if I have to take you back to kindergarten on this one, I guess the whole class will have to hear it once again."

I admired that young man for having the confidence and courage to speak out in front of his classmates, admit that he did not fully understand the burden, and ask the professor to explain it again.

He'll go places, I thought to myself.

46

In the LL.M. program, we were required to write a thesis.

I asked Professor Kathleen Sullivan to be my thesis director. I told her I was interested in writing about the duty of higher education institutions in former *de jure* states to desegregate. Was the duty to desegregate satisfied by simply removing all racial barriers to admission, or was the duty greater to include taking affirmative steps to desegregate? This was the central issue in the long-standing higher education desegregation *Ayers* case in Mississippi.

My fellow students thought my topic was passé and were surprised that someone as bright and contemporary as Professor Sullivan would have approved the topic. I worked and researched extensively, but I could not come up with anything to present to Professor Sullivan as a first draft or even an outline. Then she said to me, "Stop the research and start talking to your computer."

Words began to come to me, and soon I had a draft to submit to her. She was pleased with the draft but commented that she wished I would put more of my own opinions in the paper. I was in a difficult situation in that regard. I had an opinion – that the duty to desegregate went further than simply stopping segregation, but also required reaching out affirmatively to take all steps necessary to remove all remnants of segregation.

My opinion was not that of my federal appeals circuit court, the Fifth Circuit. As the attorney for a university in the Fifth Circuit, I did not think it wise to take a position contrary to that of my circuit.

My thesis was due on April 15, 1991. When I met Professor Sullivan outside Pound Hall to deliver it to her, she said, "You know how to hit a moving target!"

She gave me that day's front page of the *New York Times* with banner headlines: "Supreme Court agrees to hear Mississippi higher education desegregation case."

After the *Times* published the piece, I heard nothing more from my class-mates about my topic. Professor Sullivan gave me an A on my thesis, which was subsequently published by the *University of Mississippi Law Journal*.

I developed friendships with members of my LL.M. class, who were from all over the world. On one occasion, when Diann Coleman was visiting me, we invited a number of my classmates for a Southern dinner of fried chicken, peas, butter beans, fresh corn, squash casserole, cornbread, and banana pudding. As we were preparing the meal, the aroma of the fried chicken and vegetables floated all over the apartment building and onto Beacon Street below. A number of tenants of the building came by seeking an invitation to join us for the evening.

None of my classmates were from the South, and few had ever had the type of food we were serving. They ate until I was afraid they were all going to end up in the emergency room at Massachusetts General. We had a great time sitting around talking, telling stories about our hometowns and families, and eating. When they finally took their leave around midnight, I gave each one a package containing two Alka-Seltzers as a souvenir.

Throughout the year, I traveled to Mountain Top Inn in Chittendon, Vermont, where I learned to cross-country ski; Martha's Vineyard to enjoy the beauty and the charm of that island; Bar Harbor, Kennebunkport, Tenants Harbor, and Camden, Maine; Burlington, Vermont, for the University of Vermont Conference on Law and Higher Education; and Durham, New Hampshire, for a visit in the home of Margaret-Love Gathright Denman, a friend from my college days and a member of the faculty at UNH. She served us a roast cooked according to a recipe of her father's, which required putting the roast in the oven at 500 degrees for five minutes per pound, and then turning the oven off and leaving it off to finish cooking for two hours. When the oven door was opened, the roast came out cooked to perfection.

Several times I went to Hingham, Massachusetts, to visit Freemie and Bob Stone (friends from Louisville and Glendora) and enjoy fresh lobsters and corn on the cob New England-style. Stella, Mary Ann, and Jane traveled for one of our visits there, and we had Thanksgiving dinner together at the Ritz Carlton in Boston. My daughter Elizabeth and her friend Claire Bradley Ong came another time. We all had fun times together exploring the treasures of Boston and surrounding environs during those holidays.

During that year, I reconnected with Margaret-Love, but also with other friends, Susan Morehead and Tom McCraw, both Ole Miss friends and graduates. Susan and Tom held Ph.D.s in history from the University of Wisconsin. Tom was on the faculty of the Harvard Business School and the winner of a Pulitzer Prize for his book Prophets of Regulation. Susan was a graduate of the Harvard Law School and a partner in a prestigious Boston law firm. I attended a class Tom was teaching in the business school. His lecture the day I attended was on the history and development of IBM.

One of the highlights of my time in Boston came the day I met Leontyne Price at a book signing held for her at the Coop in Cambridge. I stood in line for a long time to get to meet and speak with her and have her autograph her book on *Aida* for me, my children, and the children of Jean and Jerry Jordan, conductors of the world-renowned Concert Singers at the University of Mississippi.

When I spoke to Ms. Price and she heard my voice, she immediately asked, "Where in Mississippi are you from?"

I replied Oxford. She told me that she had come to the University of Mississippi to perform in Fulton Chapel at the invitation of Chancellor Porter Fortune. I told her that I was there at her performance with my daughter Mary Ann because Chancellor Fortune had given me two tickets.

She then asked me to go over to a corner of the Coop where her aunt and other family members were gathered.

"They will be thrilled to talk with someone from Mississippi," she said, "who understands our roots."

With that, I thanked her again for her gift of music to the world and walked over to her family. We talked about our hometowns, Southern food, people and places we knew in common. The type of conversations that people in the Deep South engage in easily and frequently.

Another highlight of the year was the opportunity to attend services at Memorial Church on the Harvard campus and hear the Reverend Peter Gomes, Plumer professor of Christian morals and minister at Memorial Church, preach.

I had heard of his sermons long before arriving at Harvard but had never heard him preach or even read his sermons. I was left speechless at his eloquence.

The first sermon I heard from him began like this: "I am going to speak today about a word unknown in these environs, especially among the faculty at Harvard – the word 'humility.'"

With that, he began a powerful, spellbinding exposition on arrogance versus humility and the virtue of the latter. I bought his book containing some of his sermons and reread it frequently. It is titled *Sundays at Harvard: Sermons for an Academic Year*. I also purchased his book on the Bible entitled *The Good Book: Reading the Bible with Mind and Heart*. Both provide insights into scripture, theology, and spirituality upon which the Reverend Gomes spoke most eloquently.

My graduation in June of 1991 was a spectacular occasion with all the schools marching in from around the campus with banners flying, and all dressed in full academic regalia.

Nikita Khrushchev was the commencement speaker.

The following day, I packed my things and turned my Buick back toward the South. I recall turning and looking over my shoulder as I saw the last glimpse of the skyline of Boston, the Pru, the harbor, and the place I had loved so well.

My year at Harvard Law School recreated me mentally and spiritually. In everything I do, Harvard, Boston, and New England live on through me.

Harvard graduation, 1991

I teach better; I am more thorough; I am more intellectually stimulated. I am more compassionate and in tune to the needs of others around me. I have been more committed to making a difference in the things I think are right. I have reached out to befriend and support the gay and lesbian students on our campus and have been actively involved in supporting the efforts of individuals on the fringe.

All of this was triggered when Margaret Sims read a two-sentence letter to me from the Harvard Law School and said, "You got in."

47

Shortly after I returned from Boston, I received word that there were a large number of faculty, staff, and students gathered in the university's library who were angry and about to start a protest over the university's ignoring, in their opinion, their pleas for help and accommodations.

Chancellor Turner asked me to go over and see if I could calm the situation.

I was stunned at the anger on display. The group gathered all had disabilities of one type or another and thought the university faculty and administrators were not giving adequate attention to their needs. They told me of the need for curb cuts for those who used wheel chairs; ramps into the athletic department building and the library; prohibition of trucks, including university delivery trucks, from parking on the sidewalks blocking wheelchair movement; dedicated handicap parking places; failure of the university police to ticket and even tow vehicles parked in the few handicap parking places we did have; resistance by certain faculty to giving extended time for tests to students with learning disabilities; and failure to provide sign language interpreters for classes in which students with significant hearing impairments were enrolled.

I sensed the urgency of the situation.

I returned as soon as possible to the chancellor's office and told him the situation was about to get out of hand. I suggested that he immediately create a Chancellor's Committee on Disability Compliance, seat me as the chair, and let me choose the twelve members of the committee, at least nine of whom must have a disability.

I asked that he allocate $250,000 a year for us to use to make the campus more compliant with the American with Disabilities Act (ADA) and more user-friendly to our constituency.

He agreed.

We convened the Chancellor's Committee on Disability Compliance and discussed the various issues the group had with the condition and accommodations on campus. We decided to list all the problem areas and then hold a vote on how we thought the $250,000 should be spent. I thought we should install an elevator in Bryant Hall, which would permit students who used wheelchairs or crutches to reach the third floor of the building, where most student plays were performed. My recommendation would have taken almost all of the money allocated for the year. The committee disagreed with me and voted eleven to one to allocate the funds to improving the sidewalks on the campus.

To persuade me that they were right in their view, the committee asked me to conduct an experiment. I agreed, but I was not a stranger to disability.

When I returned from summer camp to Louisville in August of 1953, I was rejoicing to be with my hometown friends. A few days after we arrived home, I awakened one morning freezing but burning hot at the same time. I could not get up and could not call for help. Finally, my parents opened the door to my room and witnessed my distress.

Polio was ravaging the country and had hit the southern part of Virginia particularly hard. I could see the terror in their faces as they called Dr. David Richardson, a local physician, whose daughter had been recently diagnosed with polio.

Dr. Richardson found my symptoms the same as his daughter's and concluded that polio had attacked me.

Louisville was terrified. A big yellow police tape was placed around our home with QUARANTINE written in large letters. Anyone who had been in contact with me had to be inoculated with gamma globulin and was told to stay away from our house. For weeks, I was confined to my home with little to do but watch soap operas on our new television.

The diagnosis was never conclusively confirmed. I was one of the fortunate ones who had a mild case of polio that ran its course without permanent paralysis.

Polio left me with little lasting effects. That was not the case with Ed Connell and my friend Money Luckett. Money was confined to an iron lung for 50 years, until a local Clarksdale businessman, Jon Levingston, who had become a frequent visitor and good friend of Money's, began to wonder if there were newer, smaller devices that could provide Money the ability to breathe air into her body. Jon contacted friends and friends of friends to try and locate a doctor specializing in post-polio syndrome to assess Money's situation and provide guidance and direction for her future. Fortunately, Jon found a doctor in St. Louis at the Jewish Hospital, now known as the Barnes-Jewish Hospital, who agreed to see Money and evaluate her medical condition.

Rives Neblett, a successful attorney and a pilot, offered to fly Money to the hospital for an evaluation. Her mother, Kellye, and Jon removed most of the back seats of the plane, strapped Money into a small, single-engine Beechcraft Bonanza, and took-off for St. Louis to try to give her a better life. Money was thrilled with the flight and with the results of the evaluation and recommendations for her future care and existence.

Together they learned of a new breathing device that actively pumped air into Money's lungs. The device was small and portable, with a tube that delivered air into her mouth and could be attached to a mask that was strapped to her head for night-time use. As Jon described it: "This miraculous invention had the potential to free Money from the Iron Lung and, more importantly, during the day, from her bed and her room. Money could become mobile."

After successfully investing some of Money's funds with the help of Rives Neblett, Jon bought a motorized chair and a new Ford van equipped with a lift to safely and comfortably transport her in and out of it. With a driver and a caregiver, Money was able to leave her home and travel throughout the Southern states. She particularly enjoyed going to Destin, Florida, a popular spot for many Deltans. She attended concerts and art galleries and went shopping and to the grocery store.

Money lived a life of uncommon achievement. She described herself as "one tough cookie." Twice, she suffered bouts with cancer, which resulted in mastectomies, one under only a local anesthetic because of pulmonary limitations. She had little tolerance for people who crumbled under fire. "Disabled doesn't mean unable," she said. "With a little help, you can do anything."

The members of the Chancellor's Committee on Disability Compliance asked me to take a ride in an automated wheelchair from the Lyceum to Coulter Hall, which required me to cross University Avenue to the Alumni House, and then return back to the Lyceum building, without getting out of the chair.

My interest in persons with disabilities started years ago when I attended St. George's Episcopal Church in Clarksdale shortly after Bill and I were married. St. George's sponsored a program for children with disabilities — blindness, deafness, Down Syndrome. I gained some insight into their meaningful, but challenging lives, but I had never really "walked in their shoes."

So I agreed with their request. I pledged that I would not get out of the chair no matter how difficult the challenge.

The first challenge was the absence of curb cuts. When I arrived at the University Avenue Bridge, I could not cross the street because I could not get off the sidewalk. When I finally conquered that challenge, the motor on the chair stopped in the middle of the street, and I could not restart it. Classes were changing; traffic was stalled because of my being stuck in the middle of the street; horns were blowing, and students were shouting at me to get out of the way.

Finally, a UPD officer came along and helped me get up on the sidewalk in front of the Alumni house, across rough places in the sidewalks, and I made my way back to the Lyceum without having broken my pledge. After that experience, I was a convinced believer that the sidewalks were our top priority.

The Chancellor's Committee on Disability Compliance remained active and the chancellor's commitment of funds intact. Through the work of Steve Mauldin, Martha White, Dr. Ed Woods, Lori Sneed, and others, the campus was transformed: curb cuts were installed where needed; braille signs were placed on all buildings; door handles were changed to be more easily used by those with arthritic hands; bathroom stalls were widened, and interpreters were employed to assist hearing-impaired students and staff. By the end of my time chairing this committee, the group gave me a whistle. It was inscribed in braille, thanking me for my leadership.

48

The Phi Beta Sigma and Beta Theta Pi racial incidents took place during one of the re-occurring debates over the Confederate flag.

At a meeting of the board of directors of the Ole Miss Alumni Association on October 27, 1991, the association unanimously adopted a resolution asking fans and alumni not to bring the Confederate flag to Ole Miss athletic events. Dr. Sansing reported that George Hewes, president of the alumni association, said the board made this recommendation because the flag projected a negative national image of the university. Raymond Brown, president-elect and a former great Ole Miss quarterback, endorsed the resolution.

He said, "Because the flag makes it difficult for the university to recruit scholars, faculty, and athletes."

This resolution was followed a year later by Chancellor Turner's appointment of Rob Evans, the first black head coach of a major sport at Ole Miss. Evans' success in raising the university's basketball program to national prominence and the appointment of Rod Barnes, also black, as assistant coach had a positive impact on the public image of Ole Miss.

Chancellor Turner had accomplished much to enhance accessibility (actual and psychological) to Ole Miss for African American students. He made the case for private funding; he garnered support from Mississippi's powerful Congressional delegation for federal funding of research centers, and he hired African Americans in prominent positions on campus.

But perhaps his most visible act — at least from the standpoint of alumni — was to save the Grove, the shady nine-plus acre plot of land in the center of the campus that is home to majestic oaks, mysterious elms, and magnolia trees.

Before Chancellor Turner arrived, the Grove was closed on rainy football-game days, a practice that was resented — and not followed — by many fans. When the cars of disobeying fans were mired down in mud, the physical plant would have to bring in heavy tractors to pull them out of the Grove, causing significant damage to the trees and expense to the university.

Paul Hale, director of the physical plant, was advised that the Grove was dying because of the weight of the cars parked in the Grove on game days and the damage they did to the roots of the trees.

Chancellor Turner realized that most alumni, who professed powerful love for the Grove, did not notice the damage taking place and that the Grove was dying. There were large areas without trees. He directed the planting of sixteen large oaks trees in the Grove, acquired an irrigation system, and created a "Save the Grove Campaign" to pay for it all. After a particularly rainy Saturday game day in 1991, Chancellor Turner ordered the Grove closed to cars completely. The outcry was loud, and Chancellor Turner was told to go back to Texas (and other places). As time went on and alumni saw how great it was to have more space in the Grove and not to have to worry about their children being run over by cars barreling to "their" spot, he began to receive many letters apologizing and thanking him for making the right call.

Turner told me, "When I see the Grove with TV announcers talking about how many people are packed into its shady nine acres, I just smile."

49

On May 17, 1994, Chancellor Turner called me to his office. He was discouraged. And I had seen this look on his face before.

"I can't believe this is happening again," he said.

The NCAA had sent another official inquiry letter informing Chancellor Turner that allegations of violations of association rules had been made again involving the university's football program.

Chancellor Turner faced the same decision regarding whether to outsource the investigation and response or to handle it in-house. He again decided to handle the mater internally, believing it was the university's responsibility to investigate and respond to accusations alleged against it of wrongdoing.

This time, he appointed a committee comprised of Dr. Les Wyatt, executive assistant to the chancellor, as chair; Professor of Law Tom Mason; Dr. Max Williams; and me. Again, we divided the investigation responsibilities among the committee members.

The alleged violations this time were similar to those made in the previous 1983-84 investigation, although this time they were more serious because they involved the same program (football) under the same coach (Brewer) and were of a lurid nature involving alcohol, strip clubs, topless dancers, offers of money, and plane tickets.

Dr. Wyatt traveled to Las Vegas and California to interview Jason Sehorn, a prospective student-athlete who had allegedly been offered cash as well as plane tickets for his mother and girlfriend to come to Ole Miss to see him play. Dr. Wyatt interviewed others with knowledge of the allegations surrounding this prospective student-athlete to ascertain what they had heard from him regarding what he had or had not been offered to make an official visit to campus and to eventually play football at Ole Miss. I then traveled to Rome, Georgia, to interview another prospective student-athlete from California regarding alleged offers to entice him to visit Ole Miss.

Dr. Wyatt and I together interviewed several alumni who had allegedly made improper offers of cash and other benefits to encourage prospective student-athletes to make an official visit to the Ole Miss campus and commit to attend the university.

Dr. Wyatt returned to Ole Miss after his initial investigations.

"Mary Ann," he said, "we're going to lose, and we're going to lose big." He paused for a moment and added, "These things all happened."

Dr. Williams interviewed several alums regarding improper offers of money and clothes they had made to prospective student athletes. I traveled to LSU to interview a student-athlete there, to Mississippi State, to the LaFont Inn in Pascagoula, and to numerous high school gyms, coaches' offices, and locker rooms. The travel on the part of team members was extensive and exhausting.

As in the first investigation, I wrote the response and circulated it to all team members and Chancellor Turner for suggestions and comments. We then submitted it to the NCAA.

On July 11, 1994, Warner Alford, my old college friend, resigned as athletics director.

"This is twice," he said, "under my watch."

Warner believed a change in leadership was best for the university. This was painful for him, as well as for all of us who admired and respected him. The university provided Warner $100,000 in severance pay.

The following day, Head Football Coach Billy Brewer was fired.

On August 31, 1994, the university disassociated two representatives of its athletics interests and prohibited them from having any further involvement with the athletic program or attending any athletic events.

The hearing before the Committee on Infractions took place in Kansas City on September 30, 1994.

On November 17, 1994, the Committee on Infractions released its findings of violations and penalties to be imposed, which included a public reprimand and censure of the university; four years of probation; a requirement that the university develop a comprehensive athletics compliance education program with annual reports to the Committee on Infractions during the period of probation; prohibition from televising any football games during the 1995 season; reduction by twelve in the number of initial financial aid awards in football for the 1995-96 and 1996-97 academic years; reduction by sixteen in the number of permissible official visits in football during the same two academic years; recertification of current athletics policies and practices; disassociation of two representatives of the institution's athletics interests; and a show-cause requirement on the former head football coach, Coach Brewer, for four years.

The university appealed the finding of the Committee on Infractions involving an offer to prospective student-athlete Jason Sehorn of cash and free airline tickets for the prospect's mother and girlfriend. We also asked for a reduction in the penalties involving football grants-in-aid and official visits.

The Infractions Appeals Committee heard oral arguments on the appeal in Houston, Texas, on March 1, 1995.

Mike Slive was chair of the Infractions Appeals Committee. We thought we presented our case well and were optimistic that our appeal would be upheld.

The committee denied both of the appeals, and the sanctions were imposed.

In the spring of 1995, Chancellor Turner flew to Lawrence, Kansas. He was one of three finalists for the chancellor position at the University of Kansas. He and the other candidates were being interviewed by the Kansas Board of Regents.

While Chancellor Turner was in Kansas, Billy Brewer's attorney filed a lawsuit in Oxford, Mississippi, at the Lafayette County Courthouse, against the University of Mississippi, the College Board, and Gerald Turner personally, for wrongful termination. The suit sought lost compensation and damages for pain and suffering, as well as punitive damages.

Turner was named individually in the suit because he personally handled Brewer's dismissal. The claim stated that Turner fired Brewer without affording the coach due process.

I hated to see Chancellor Turner's tenure end on this note, but we knew he was interviewing for top positions at Ohio State, SMU, University of Kansas, and other universities.

Under Turner's tenure, enrollment rose from 8,715 in 1984 to 11,033 in 1992. Much of the enrollment growth was from out-of-state students. His initiatives moved black student enrollment in graduate school from less than 20 to about 100 in two years. In less than ten years, the number of black students at the university nearly doubled from 536 in 1984 to approximately 1,000 in 1992.

African American faculty and administrators appointed by Turner included Thomas Wallace, associate vice chancellor for student life; Ken Gibson, track coach; and Louis Westerfield, dean of the law school.

Working with Chancellor Turner was a Camelot time for me. I admired and respected him and found him to be energized, intelligent, and focused on making Ole Miss a better university. He was a great university president. I knew from the beginning that with his youth and abilities, he would not stay with us long. I was grateful we kept him for eleven years.

I had no idea who would succeed Chancellor Turner. I doubted anyone could live up to the standard he set, but someone would.

IX
University Attorney: The Khayat Years

50

There are moments of near perfection. Times when the right person for the right job at the right time intersect. One of those moments began when Robert Khayat was the unanimous selection by the Board of Trustees of State Institutions of Higher Learning to serve as the 15th chancellor of the University of Mississippi.

When Robert's name emerged as a consensus candidate for the position, Mississippi's two United States senators, the legal profession, the business community, the alumni association, the student body, the university faculty, and the general public universally applauded his appointment.

Robert graduated from Ole Miss in 1960. He was an All-SEC football and baseball student-athlete, an Academic All-American in football, a member of the 1960 University of Mississippi Hall of Fame, an honor graduate of the university's law school, a member of the university's law school faculty, the recipient of an LL.M. from the Yale University School of Law, president of the NCAA Foundation, and vice chancellor for university affairs at Ole Miss. He was an All-Pro kicker in the NFL (he twice led the nation in scoring for kickers). Robert was also one of the two freshmen in 1956 who took the last pastries at the Methodist church before I had a chance to impress Dan Jordan.

During his interview with the IHL Board in 1995, Nan Baker, president of the Board of Trustees, opened the interview with one question.

"Dr. Khayat," she asked, "what is your vision for the University of Mississippi?" The soon-to-be Chancellor Khayat looked around the room at the other IHL board members and replied, "To be — and to be perceived as — one of America's great public universities."

On his first official day as chancellor, he arrived at his office, took a yellow legal pad, and outlined the major issues facing the university: enrollment, increased private support, efficient management, and morale.

He turned the page on the legal pad on which he was writing and wrote: Goals.

He scribbled: *unite our faculty, staff, students, and alumni to work toward common goals, increase enrollment on the Oxford campus to 12,000 by the year 2000, continue development of the Medical Center and the expansion of healthcare services in the state, increase our endowment to $100 million by the year 2000, increase the number of Ph.D.s awarded annually to 100+, increase library holdings to 1,000,000+ volumes by the year 2000, increase faculty and staff salaries to regional averages, establish a leadership position for our technology initiative, develop a teacher evaluation plan for the IHL system, and collaborate with other pubic educational institutions.*

As he looked over the list, Chancellor Khayat knew this was a tall order that would require an extraordinary effort on behalf of administration, faculty, staff, students, and alumni, but most of all a great leadership team.

Chancellor Khayat said that he wanted team members who would inspire and challenge him. And each other.

He asked Dr. Gerald Walton to delay his retirement and remain for three more years as vice chancellor for academic affairs. He tapped Dr. Andy Mullins to serve as assistant to the chancellor. He asked Rex Deloach, and later Johnny Williams, to serve as vice chancellor for administration and finance. He sought out his long-time law school colleague Carolyn Staton to act as associate vice chancellor for academic affairs. Dr. Alice Clark was picked to serve as vice chancellor for research and sponsored programs. Thomas Wallace was chosen as vice chancellor for student life.

Chancellor Khayat persuaded Sue Keiser to come on board as assistant to the chancellor. He asked Pete Boone to continue to serve as athletics director. Don Frugé served as CEO and president of the University of Mississippi Foundation.

I was asked to stay on as university attorney and team member to provide legal advice and assistance as needed by the chancellor.

51

From the day I started work as university attorney in 1982, I was the only lawyer employed full-time by the administration, but I had superb assistance, first from Ginger Newsome and then Margaret Sims.

Ginger was so capable that she was quickly stolen away from me by Dr. Tom Meredith and then later on by Chancellor Turner himself. Margaret Sims filled Ginger's position and was a loyal, dedicated, and capable legal assistant.

Margaret also had another quality that proved invaluable. She made it nearly impossible for my four daughters to get through to me unless she was convinced that there was a true "emergency."

For that approach, valued highly by me, my daughters affectionately called her "the Colonel." All of her military skills were called upon to deal with the high drama that arose in a family with four daughters. She had to field dozens of questions, such as "Can I have a spend-the-night party Friday night? Can I charge a sweater at Neilson's?" and referee disagreements, such as "Stella wore my white blouse without my permission," and "Mary Ann is looking at me funny."

In the fall of 1995, I decided to hire a law clerk.

That same fall, a young law student, Roy Percy, from Greenville, Mississippi, met my daughter, Mary Ann Connell, at a social function. Roy, apparently, was quite taken with her beauty and charm.

The next day, at the law school, Roy learned that the university attorney — Mary Ann Connell — was looking for a law clerk. He immediately called the university attorney's office and asked for an appointment. Margaret scheduled him for a Tuesday afternoon at 2:00 p.m.

Roy arrived at the appointed time. He wore jeans and a casual pull-over fleece. He threw his back pack on the floor and said to Margaret, "Tell Mary Ann that Roy is here."

Margaret bristled. "Roy," she said, "do you have a last name?"

"Percy," he told her.

"I will tell *Ms.* Connell that *Mr.* Percy is here for his appointment."

With that, I walked into the reception area and met him.

"Mr. Percy," I said, "I am Mary Ann Connell."

The look on his face was complete disappointment. He had expected to see the young, beautiful woman he had met a few nights earlier, not her 63-year-old mother.

"Let us go talk about your qualifications and interest in a clerkship in this office," I said, as I led him to my office.

Mr. Percy was well-qualified for the law clerk position. He had attended Episcopal High School in Alexandria, Virginia, held an undergraduate degree from the University of Virginia in history, and was in his third year of law school at Ole Miss as a top student.

After our interview, I offered him the position as one of my law clerks. He accepted and did a fine job.

A year later, in 1996, the IHL Board approved funds for a second university attorney. We had a large pool of applicants. A number came from large, prestigious firms in Jackson and Memphis.

"I am your man," one applicant from a Jackson firm said. "I cannot think of a better life than working on campus and going out every afternoon to watch the Rebels practice."

I knew he was not going to be a good fit.

One of the applicants was a young man named Cal Mayo.

Cal was a graduate of the University of Mississippi with a major — and Taylor Medal — in accountancy. Cal was a graduate of the University of Virginia School of Law. He had worked as an associate with Butler Snow in Jackson, one of Mississippi's largest and most prestigious law firms.

Cal was, by far, the best qualified applicant. He was offered the position, and he accepted.

In short order, I turned most matters involving athletics and litigation over to Cal. He excelled in both areas. He proved to have been the right person for the job.

Cal Mayo and Mary Ann at the
NACUA conference, circa 1996

Cal began work in our office on January 2, 1996. Twenty days later, on January 22, 1996, we began an age discrimination lawsuit in federal court in Oxford. A woman my age, with whom I had attended Ole Miss in the 1950s, twice applied for a position as a legal writing specialist in the law school. The law faculty concurred on both occasions that she was not as well qualified for the position as other younger candidates.

The faculty thought the work experiences of the younger candidates were more relevant for teaching the skills law students needed than were the qualifications of the older candidate.

Angered by the faculty's decisions, the older woman filed suit claiming age discrimination.

The trial took place over three days in the federal courthouse in Oxford, Mississippi. Jim Waide, an outstanding trial lawyer from Tupelo, Mississippi, represented the plaintiff.

The university lost the jury trial on one of the claims. We immediately asked the judge to grant the university a JNOV (judgment notwithstanding the verdict). We argued that the plaintiff had not presented evidence sufficient to rebut the university's solid reasons for selecting the younger woman over her.

The judge declined the request. We appealed to the Fifth Circuit Court of Appeals.

We had called a number of law professors as witnesses. They had built a good record at the trial court level. Their testimony that their preferred candidate's job responsibilities as a permanent federal law clerk for four and a half years, her brief-writing experience, and strong letters of recommendation from three federal court judges with whom she had worked indicated she had the qualifications and skills to teach legal writing to our law students.

The Fifth Circuit Court of Appeals reversed and rendered the trial court's decision. They also issued a strong legal opinion favorable to the university and helpful to all our public universities as they dealt with age discrimination claims.

A natural litigator, Cal had done an excellent job in the law school age discrimination trial. He also adjusted quickly to the culture of the academic community and was well-respected on the university's campus.

Cal reviewed the more complex contracts, lease purchase agreements, federal research contracts, and he played an important role in negotiating coaches' contracts.

Cal and I worked well together.

52

Chancellor Khayat and Andy Mullins began an aggressive schedule of speeches, recruitment, and fundraising trips around the state.

The chancellor and Don Frugé steadily called on alumni and potential donors not only in Mississippi, but nationally.

One of the first major gifts Chancellor Khayat facilitated was from Larry and Susan Martindale.

Larry went to Ole Miss on a basketball scholarship. After Larry graduated in the 1950s, he joined the army. He served for three years, was discharged, and took a job cooking at a Waffle House. He eventually rose to be a manager. Before long, Larry acquired ownership in one Waffle House. And then another. Soon, Larry owned a string of the restaurants.

Then, in a strange twist of fate, Larry went from buying Waffle House restaurants to owning Ritz-Carlton hotels. And in the process, he and Susan acquired great wealth.

Larry's mother, who lived with her son and his wife during these young, hard-working years, always reminded him of the debt he owed the University of Mississippi.

"Larry," she would ask, "have you repaid Ole Miss for your basketball scholarship?" "Mama," he would answer, "someday I will do that — when I have gotten my family started and my businesses successfully under way."

From his days as a Ritz-Carlton owner, Larry understood the importance of attention to detail. He and Susan, having seen our relatively unkempt campus, made a large contribution to beautification and upkeep of the university's grounds.

In appreciation for their generosity, the renovated old gym, where Larry played basketball for Ole Miss in the 1950s, was named "Martindale Hall."

On the day of dedication of the renovated building, the street in front of Martindale was closed, and a stage was erected in the middle of the street.

A large crowd gathered for the ceremony.

Larry talked about how he was able to come to college because of a basketball scholarship valued at about $3,500 a year. He had come from humble means and could not have attended college without this scholarship.

On the day Martindale Hall was dedicated, Chancellor Khayat thanked Susan and Larry for the significant sums of money they had given to renovation of the old gym and beautification of the campus grounds.

Larry rose to speak.

He looked up at the heavens, pointed a finger upward, and said: "Mama, I hope you are happy. My debt is now paid in full."

Tears filled his eyes. And mine.

Chancellor Khayat was an incredible fund-raiser. Stories of his powers of persuasion took on almost supernatural proportions. He raised millions for an honors college, for faculty salaries, for academic programs. He had secured pledges for nearly $100 million in his first two years as chancellor.

In late 1995, Chancellor Khayat called U.S. Magistrate Judge Allan Alexander's office to schedule a visit with her. When she received the message that he had called to set up a meeting, she said to her staff, "Lock up your purses and wallets. He is on the way!"

53

On October 13, 1996, Chancellor Khayat traveled to Washington, D.C. He met with Dr. Douglas Foard, executive secretary of Phi Beta Kappa, at an office located on Dupont Circle.

Chancellor Khayat was direct.

"Douglas," he asked, "why do you think Ole Miss has been denied membership in Phi Beta Kappa in the past?"

Dr. Foard didn't answer right away. He asked Chancellor Khayat questions. The two men talked for nearly two hours.

At the end of the meeting, Dr. Foard suggested several barriers standing between Ole Miss and the opportunity to shelter a Phi Beta Kappa chapter.

The list of obstacles, in Dr. Foard's opinion, included library holdings, faculty salaries, academic standards, and NCAA probation.

Then Dr. Foard cleared his throat and offered Chancellor Khayat one more opinion.

"And, of course," he said, "you'll have to address racial issues, including the university's association with the Confederate flag."

None of us could have ever imagined the impact of Dr. Foard's demand.

54

In 1993, Dick Crockett, president of NACUA and General Counsel at Syracuse University, called to ask if I would serve a three-year term on the NACUA Board of Directors. I was flattered that I would be asked to serve in this capacity and immediately accepted the invitation.

We had many difficult decisions to make. Each required careful deliberation. We determined how to affix dues for member institutions and associate members. We faced whether members representing certain associations, such as the NCAA and AAUP with sometimes conflicting interests with NACUA, should be allowed membership. Whether to permit attendance by the press gave rise to hours of discussion and debate, as did the increasing participation of private attorneys presenting at the annual conferences and workshops.

For me personally, one of the hardest decisions was whether to discontinue providing free hard copies of the *West Education Law Reporter* and its supplements to the membership, or to instead distribute these materials electronically. The same issue arose with respect to distribution of *The Journal of College and University Law* electronically. I understood the economies of these decisions and that a younger generation prefers reading from the computer screen, but I do not. This was truly a generational issue that was decided correctly to go electronic in the best interest of the association financially.

In 1995, I was nominated to be second vice president of the association, a position which was a one-year learning period before becoming first vice president and chair of the annual conference program committee. During that year, I observed and worked with Andy Schaffer, general counsel at New York University, and learned much that helped me the following year when I was in charge of the program for the annual conference in Seattle. The year I served as first vice president was a busy one. The planning of the program, identifying topics and speakers was a huge responsibility. I was chair of a remarkable group of attorneys who worked together well to put on a program in Seattle that I thought turned out to be excellent.

The Seattle conference in 1997 was special for many of us east of the Mississippi River who had never traveled to the northwest and had the opportunity to enjoy the city of Seattle. All went perfectly at the conference until on the eve of my presentation with Robin Green and Beverly Ledbetter, general counsel at Brown University, on "How to Conduct an NCAA Infractions Investigation In-House," I came down with a terrible case of food poisoning, a malady that afflicted a number of attendees who had dined at the same restaurant the evening before. On the morning of my presentation, I called Robin and said that there was no way I could leave my hotel room and asked if she and Beverly could cover the entire program in my absence. In true NACUA style, both Robin and Beverly immediately responded "Yes," and the show went on.

The following year, 1998-1999, was my term as president of NACUA. One of the primary responsibilities of the president is to appoint committees. Important to me was gaining more involvement in the work of NACUA by representatives of large, competitive institutions. Bill Kauffman of St. Louis University was first vice president that year and would succeed me as president. He came to Oxford, Mississippi, and met with me in my office for hours going over the membership and identifying people to appoint to committees who would increase NACUA's diversity in race, gender, large/small institutions, and public/private institutions. I made personal phone calls to each person appointed to a committee to ask if he or she would be interested in serving and to explain what the committee responsibility entailed. Through those calls, I made many new NACUA friends.

The University of Mississippi fielded a women's basketball team from 1922 to 1931, but we offered no athletics programs for women from 1931 to 1974.

Mary Ann and Bill Kauffman

The university re-established women's basketball in 1974. A varsity women's tennis team was formed in 1975. We added slow pitch softball in 1978. Women's track and field (indoor, outdoor, and cross-country) and golf were both added in 1986. And in 1995, we added women's soccer.

Title IX of the Education Amendments of 1972 (commonly referred to as "Title IX") is a federal law that prohibits discrimination on the basis of gender by educational institutions that receive federal funds. The law was passed by Congress after years of wrestling with the issue of equitable treatment of male and female college athletes.

While some universities offered sports opportunities for women prior to Title IX, most did not.

During the first 20 years after passage of Title IX, there was almost no level of enforcement of the law by the federal government. But in 1992, *Time* magazine featured a cover with a big question mark and the caption: "What ever happened to Title IX?"

It was the beginning of a series of gender discrimination lawsuits against universities.

The Fifth Circuit Court of Appeals in *Pederson v. Louisiana State University* ruled that LSU had engaged in "systematic, intentional, differential treatment of women" and affirmed the trial court's ruling that the university had violated Title IX. The court appeared to serve warning on universities that do not provide equivalent opportunities for men and women that serious consequences will lie.

Case after case was decided in favor of the women plaintiffs, who sued for equal playing and practice time, equal facilities, equal pay for coaches, equitable allocation of financial resources and scholarships, and equivalent benefits and services, such as provision of medical and training facilities, housing and dining facilities, and publicity efforts dedicated to their sports.

The University of Mississippi was already under way in its efforts to become more compliant with Title IX before these cases were decided. In 1991, the university participated in the NCAA certification pilot survey. In 1994, Chancellor Gerald Turner appointed a Title IX compliance review committee, which I chaired. We inspected athletic facilities, developed questionnaires and a survey seeking information from both students and coaches, analyzed extensive data, formulated findings of fact, and made both tangible and intangible recommendations for improvement at the University of Mississippi in the area of gender equity.

We submitted the report of the Title IX compliance review committee with the following recommendations:

- Develop an institutional plan for addressing recommendations of this committee and issues of gender equity in the future;
- Review annually the efforts of the university to comply with the recommendations of the committee and submit a report to the chancellor before March 1 of each year;
- Designate an individual within the Department of Intercollegiate Athletics to disseminate information on Title IX compliance to student-athletes, coaches, and administrators, and staff members;
- Take a proactive role in supporting programs for women in intramural and club sports;
- Make aggressive efforts to recruit and hire more women coaches, administrators, and staff members;
- Achieve salary equity in coaches' salaries;
- Involve women coaches, coaches of women's teams, and women administrators in the decision-making processes pertaining to intercollegiate athletics.

Ole Miss engaged in building projects that have added much to its commitment to gender equity in athletics. In 1997, the Women's Athletics Complex was completed. In 2000, the facility was named and dedicated to Jennifer and Peggie Gillom.

The NCAA began national and regional seminars to educate university presidents, athletics directors, and coaches on the legal requirements of Title IX.

In 1995, I was invited to speak at a Title IX seminar in Dallas. When I was introduced to the audience of mainly athletic directors and coaches of men's sports (mainly football), I was booed.

During the Q & A that followed, questions were posited as to why women wanted to kill football, which provides the financial support for all other programs.

55

In addition to my duties as university attorney and president of NAC-UA, I continued teaching. After my stint as an instructor at the law school, I began teaching business law — a required class for all business and accountancy students.

In business law, I covered a wide range of subjects from contracts to torts, and criminal law to constitutional law.

In one class in the mid-1990s, I was explaining the concept of the separation of church and state. I explained the United States Supreme Court decision regarding state-sponsored prayer in public schools.

One of my best students, Cooper Manning, son of Ole Miss football great Archie Manning, sat on the back row in one of the classrooms in Conner Hall.

"Ms. Connell," Mr. Manning said, "what is wrong with a teacher leading a prayer in school? This is a Christian nation."

"The law is well-settled in this area," I explained. "It is not the business of public schools to sponsor prayer in a school setting or at school activities," I said.

"We were founded as a Christian nation," Mr. Manning argued. "We should have Christian prayer."

"You may disagree with the decision," I said. "That is your right."

Then I suggested that he look around the room, at each student, and tell me what kind of prayer he thought would be appropriate for our business law class.

Mr. Manning assessed the room. He saw Asian students. Students from other countries. Many students who might not be Christian — or even religious.

As he surveyed the room, he didn't say a word.

"You are free to pray any time you want," Mr. Manning. "In fact, you may pray all through class and while you are walking across campus."

During a spring semester class the following year, when New Orleans was in full Mardi Gras celebration mode, I had a student who was prone to miss class.

One day he came to my office.

"Ms. Connell, I guess you noticed," he said, "that I have missed a few classes."

"And the mid-term exam," I added.

"Yes, ma'am."

"Your *grade* is going to notice those absences, too," I said.

"Well, you see, Ms. Connell, I have been in New Orleans all week helping my grandmother. She is a remarkable woman, but she is having a really difficult time," he told me.

"I'm so sorry," I said.

"Yeah," he said, "she depends on me to be there with her." Then, he leaned in, as if telling me a secret. "She's got prostate cancer."

"Well," I said, "she must, indeed, be a remarkable woman."

During the years I was teaching business law, I invited many of my students who could not go home for Thanksgiving to join our family for Thanksgiving dinner. One young man told me: "If I don't find something better to do, I will be there, but you will have to come to campus and pick me up."

"I will be glad to do that," I said.

"What should I wear?" he asked.

"What you would wear to church."

When I arrived at his dorm to retrieve him, the young man came out with a chartreuse suit, purple shirt, and polka-dotted tie.

He took a spot at the head of our table. He entertained us with fascinating stories of his life.

When the meal was over, he said, "I see you have a good bit of food left over."

"Yes," I said.

"Would you fix me a to-go box to take back to the dorm?"

"Of course," I told him.

I generally received positive evaluations from my business law students. The course itself was inherently interesting. It applied to everyday life.

One of my favorite comments from the evaluations was —

"Ms. Connell, you have been the best teacher I have ever had at Ole Miss. I enjoyed your class and learned a lot. I must say, however, that I saw you and several other ladies playing golf this past week at the University Golf Course and you are a lousy golfer."

56

The challenge Dr. Foard issued to Chancellor Khayat — disassociating the university from the Confederate flag — would prove more difficult than anyone could have imagined.

Though Chancellor Fortune had made clear in the early 1980s that the Confederate flag had never been an official school symbol, tens of thousands of alumni and fans continued to wave the flag at football games.

Dr. Foard could not have imagined how ingrained the symbols were in all of our lives.

My grandfather, William Augustus Strong, Sr., always dressed in a suit and bow tie. He was the epitome of a Southern gentlemen. He was born in Greenwood, Mississippi, on January 18, 1876. The Strong family lived on a plantation called "Stronghold."

Granddaddy went to work for the Gulf Mobile & Ohio Railway Company as an engineer on July 4, 1902, and became a conductor in 1904. They brought the first diesel engine to Mississippi — aptly named "The Rebel."

Granddaddy was on the board of The Jefferson Davis Shrine, which was created to preserve Beauvoir, the last home of Jefferson Davis, on the Mississippi Gulf Coast. He served on the board in the 1940s and 1950s. He was responsible for securing a $5,000 gift to the shrine from Walter D. Bellingrath, owner of Bellingrath Gardens near Mobile, Alabama, for maintaining Beauvoir.

My memories of my granddaddy are that he was loving, fun, charming, and affectionate to me. I gave him a small can of Prince Edward tobacco for his birthday and Christmas each year, and he would act as though he were thrilled to receive such a gift. I loved it when my grandmother took me by train, bus, or car to Jackson, Mississippi, to spend time at the King Edward Hotel when he was serving the railroad as a lobbyist with the Mississippi Legislature.

I adored my grandfather.

But now, I served as attorney for a university desperate to separate itself from the symbols and images that my grandfather Strong worked so hard to maintain.

My dear friend Money Luckett died on November 19, 1996. She was 59. Her funeral was held at St. Elizabeth's Catholic Church in Clarksdale with burial at Oakridge Cemetery.

A month earlier, on October 16, 1996, I received a letter from her.

Dear Mary Ann,

I am more than a dollar short and a day late, but I am close! But just in time for a conscious America. I am here to wish you an extraordinarily happy year ahead.

Whenever I stop to think, I think of an irony, which is that somehow I think you live the life I always wanted, and it greatly delights me to see how you have done it so well.

If someone has to live vicariously, why not do it with the best?

I trust all is well. I hope all is as happy as it ought to be, but with challenges here and there.

From personal experiences, if you will ever be lazy or bored, challenges make us grow.

HAPPY BIRTHDAY!

Money

Money's brother, Semmes Luckett, Jr., described Money as "always being positive." "How could you be negative or down when around her," he asked, "when she was always so upbeat?"

One of my favorite quotes from Money was —"Character isn't given."

And in typical self-deprecating fashion, she said, "It's worked out. I'm a survivor. But then anyone who has lived through a Mississippi summer is a survivor."

Clarksdale businessman Jon Levingston, perhaps, had the best thing to say about Money.

For most of her life, she fought courageously and tenaciously the ravages of a body laid waste by the polio virus. Twice she overcame cancer. She learned how to live well, despite extreme paralysis. She loved art, music, literature and travel. She sought and loved that which was the best in mankind and tolerated poorly the rest. She had passion and depth. While her infirmity caused her to face the consequent indignities of paralysis, she never succumbed to self pity. Instead, she honored the life given her by fervently embracing the best that it offered.

She was the bravest person I ever knew, and she was my best friend. I do believe that if God wrote poetry, Money was his poem.

57

When the media picked up the story that Ole Miss was reviewing its symbols, the Lyceum became a target for radicals. Chancellor Khayat and his family received death threats. The FBI was called in to secure the building. Letters and packages were opened by individuals wearing gloves and masks to protect against a potential Anthrax attack.

Chancellor Khayat, with funding provided by Jerry Hollingsworth, retained the counsel of Harold Burson, an Ole Miss graduate who also happened to be the world's leading public relations expert.

As Chancellor Khayat and Harold Burson dealt publicly with the controversy, the senior staff worked to find some solution or compromise that would prevent a complete split among our alumni — young and old, black and white, liberal and conservative, and everything in between.

Chancellor Khayat, a lawyer and a strong believer in the first amendment, would not consider banning the flag. We had to find another way.

At a meeting in 1997 — one of dozens where we brainstormed to solve the issue of fans waving Confederate flags — someone said, "Why don't we just ban sticks in the stadium."

I started to research the issue. If the issue were safety — not freedom of expression — we did have the authority to ban sticks in our stadiums.

In subsequent meetings, I stated — and reiterated — that there is no constitutional right to carry a stick or anything attached to a stick into a sports arena. There would be no evidence that the university was attempting to prohibit speech. All the university was trying to do was to protect its attendees from injury from pointed sticks and protect their ability to view the game unobstructed by banners.

After exhaustive research, Pete Boone and I recommended a "stick" ban to Chancellor Khayat. We recommended that the university ban sticks and anything attached to these sticks, as well as banners and flags exceeding 12 x 14 inches, from the stadium in the interest of safety and viewing of the athletic event.

The chancellor seemed comfortable with the guidelines and issued a public statement about the new policy on November 1, 1997:

"Consistent with the existing policy of banning umbrellas for safety reasons effective November 1, 1997, spectators will not be permitted to bring sticks or other pointed objects to University of Mississippi athletic events."

Signs posted outside the stadium in November 1997 read:

• No containers or alcoholic beverages
• No umbrellas
• No flags larger than 12" x 14"
• All personal items subject to search

None of us knew if the stick ban would work.

The first game with the ban in effect was November 6, 1997, against Arkansas. The students and alumni were in large part cooperative. The policy worked. At the LSU game a few weeks earlier, it appeared that the entire stadium was a sea of Confederate flags. Now, there were none.

58

In 1997, Cal saw an opportunity to start his own law firm in Oxford. When he told me that he planned to resign his associate university attorney position, I was devastated. He was a joy to work with and was such an outstanding lawyer that I knew that I, and the entire university community, would miss him.

We began advertising for his position.

Cal participated with me in the interviews and in the ultimate decision to hire Lee Tyner, a practicing attorney with Butler Snow in Jackson, Mississippi. Lee earned his Bachelor of Arts degree in economics and history from the University of Mississippi and his juris doctor from the University of Virginia.

Lee proved to be the perfect choice for me. He has a brilliant legal mind, a strong work ethic, and a true understanding of what higher education is and should be. He, his wife, Susan, and their family moved to Oxford, and Lee began work in the university attorney's office in November 1998. Lee assumed many of the responsibilities Cal had previously held.

On Lee's first day of work in the university attorney's office, I asked him to meet with a group of men from Houston, Texas, to negotiate a highly complicated contract through which the Houston-based company would re-engineer the university's energy savings program. He worked hours and weeks on this agreement, which ultimately spawned two projects that saved the university hundreds of thousands of dollars over the next five years. First, we undertook renovations that generated energy savings that paid for those renovations and also paid for an additional chilled water loop/ mechanical plant. A subsidiary or division of Reliant Energy (now Centerpoint Energy) was our primary partner in that project. Second, in a separate project that resulted from ideas generated as a part of the original RFP, we also built a back-up power generation plant so that we could move to interruptible power. At that time, we could buy power at a much lower rate if TVA could interrupt our power on occasion during peak loads.

Richard Barrett, an avowed white supremacist who had twice run for governor, filed suit against the university for an incident that took place a year earlier.

Mr. Barrett had attended the Arkansas game in November 1997 with two companions who possessed a concealed 3' x 5' Confederate flag and attempted to display the flag inside the stadium.

Officers of the University Police Department reminded them of the new policies and ordered them to take the flag down. The men refused to comply. The officers called UPD Captain Calvin Sellers, who warned the men that failure to comply would result in their arrest. They removed the flag.

Barrett asked that the university allow him to display a 3' x 5' Confederate flag at the next home game, scheduled for November 22, 1997. The university refused.

Barrett filed suit against the University of Mississippi and the Board of Trustees of State Institutions of Higher Learning.

The university filed a motion to dismiss pursuant to the 11th Amendment to the U.S. Constitution, which grants immunity to the state and its agencies from suit for money damages against them in federal court without their consent. The university and the board had not consented to the suit. Barrett amended his suit to add Chancellor Khayat and various members of the College Board.

Judge Neal Biggers, finding that members of the board played no role in implementing the stick ban or had any duty to consider the stick ban policy, dismissed the board and its members in both their individual and official capacities. He also dismissed Barrett's claims for money damages against the University of Mississippi and Chancellor Khayat in his official capacity under 11th Amendment immunity, leaving only Barrett's claims against the university officials in their official capacities for injunctive relief.

The suit moved forward. The university moved for summary judgment. Judge Biggers granted the motion and wrote a "brief, but more than adequate opinion," complimented by First Amendment scholar and former president of the University of Virginia, Robert O'Neil. Professor O'Neil observed that Judge Biggers first noted the paradoxical character of the Confederate battle flag and that the message conveyed by the flag "can range from endorsing demeaning and offensive racial philosophies to promoting school spirit. As beauty is in the eye of the beholder, so is the message of the flag often mainly in the perception of the observer."

In ruling in favor of the defendants, Judge Biggers "noted most helpfully and perceptively the availability of alternative expressive channels." Concluding his opinion dismissing Barrett's case, Judge Biggers wrote: "Although the bans limit the manner in which a flag may be displayed within the stadium, the court finds that this limitation upon the plaintiff's intended demonstration does not eliminate his ability to express his views elsewhere and is a reasonable time, place, and manner regulation."

We had won the battle over the Confederate flag, but the battle with Billy Brewer — a classmate, friend, and fellow teammate of Chancellor Khayat — was just beginning.

59

Cal Mayo had worked on the Billy Brewer suit when he was an associate in my office. The university hired him to continue, independently, to defend the lawsuit the former head football coach brought against the university, the IHL Board, and Gerald Turner, arising from his termination after the second NCAA investigation.

The trial began on September 27, 1999.

Judge Henry Lackey presided over the packed courthouse. He was a graduate of the University of Mississippi Law School, had practiced law in Calhoun City, and had been a circuit court judge for six years.

Brewer and his attorneys, now including Jim Waide as his trial counsel, sat at the plaintiff's table. Cal, Lee Tyner, and I sat at the defendants' table. Because I was to be a witness in the case, I ordinarily would not have been permitted to sit in the courtroom during the trial. However, Cal asked me to serve as the university's corporate representative during the trial so I was able to sit alongside Lee and Cal at the university counsels' table.

The first order of day one of the trial was jury selection. The men and women who sat on the twelve-person jury would decide the fate of the university and, to some degree, mine, since I was an integral part of the internal investigation that led to Coach Brewer's dismissal.

More than one hundred men and woman had been summoned for the jury pool. Each was given a number and seated in numerical order. Judge Lackey banged his gavel and quieted the mob of potential jurors. He then began voir dire, the process in litigation where the judge and attorneys question the potential jurors for conflicts of interest, personal beliefs, or relationships with parties associated with the lawsuit to determine their ability to render a fair and impartial verdict based only on the evidence presented during the trial.

"Is there anyone here who knows Gerald Turner personally?" Judge Lackey asked the group.

About thirty individuals raised their hands.

"Is there anyone who knows Mary Ann Connell?" About half the courtroom raised their hands.

Judge Lackey then asked the same question regarding Coach Brewer. Again, a large number held their hands up.

"Do any of you work for the University of Mississippi or have ever worked for the university," Judge Lackey asked. Again, many hands went up because the university is the largest employer in the county.

During this process, the attorneys took copious notes on what each numbered potential juror said in response to their knowledge of the parties or the issue in the trial.

Judge Lackey continued to ask about any affiliations with the university and attendance at the university. He asked about individuals who owned small businesses that would be adversely impacted by absence.

A number of the potential jurors pleaded with Judge Lackey that they simply couldn't serve on the jury because they needed to be working on their deer camps to prepare for hunting season. This explanation did not seem to carry much weight with Judge Lackey as an excuse for not being able to serve on the jury if selected.

After Judge Lackey completed his examination, Cal and Jim Waide began theirs, boring in on each potential juror to determine in their minds whether the juror would be fair or not.

At the end of the questioning, Judge Lackey, the attorneys, Coach Brewer, and I all adjourned to Judge Lackey's chambers to begin the final jury selection process. Jim Waide asked that each juror who knew Chancellor Turner or me personally be excused for cause. Cal objected strenuously, but Judge Lackey granted Jim's request. I watched as the names of dozens of acquaintances and co-workers at the university were stricken from the list.

By the time Judge Lackey had whittled down the pool of potential jurors, a few dozen individuals — primarily minority — remained in the jury pool.

The final jury consisted of nine African American men and women and three individuals, only one of whom had any affiliation with Ole Miss.

I wasn't sure the jury accurately represented the demographics of Lafayette County. But I felt certain we had all the evidence we needed to justify Billy Brewer's termination.

60

The trial began.

Jim Waide called sixteen witnesses. Each painted a picture of Coach Brewer as a poor white boy who grew up in Columbus, Mississippi, near a black neighborhood, where he was often the only white boy playing pick-up football with black children.

The witnesses depicted Billy Brewer as a coach who loved his black players and treated them kindly and with respect. And there was no question that his players loved him.

Many of his witnesses admitted they had given money, clothes, and gifts to players. They testified that what they did was right whether it violated NCAA rules or not.

In their minds, giving money and gifts and providing transportation was simply helping poor boys move ahead in life through football.

"It's their only way out of poverty!" one witness exclaimed.

The jury seemed sympathetic to Coach Brewer.

Early in his case, Mr. Waide turned to Judge Lackey and announced, "We call to the witness stand Mary Ann Connell."

61

I had prepared to be a witness for the university, but I was surprised to be called as an adverse witness by the plaintiff so early in the trial. I was nervous and did not perform as well as either Cal or I would have liked. Jim was wearing me down with his relentless queries about the NCAA rules, details of the investigation of each alleged wrong-doer. I felt that Jim was framing each question to insinuate that I had a personal vendetta against Coach Brewer, which was not the case at all. I had simply done my job.

Finally, after many days of testimony, Jim Waide rested their case. Judge Lackey recessed court. The following day, Cal Mayo would begin his case for the university.

The biggest legal issue in the case revolved around the burden of proof. *Did the university have grounds for dismissal of Billy Brewer? Put another way, Did the university have to prove that Coach Brewer committed all the violations of NCAA rules with which he was charged?" or "Could the University prove only that it had a reasonable belief that he had knowingly and willingly violated these rules?*

The university maintained that it reasonably believed Coach Brewer seriously and deliberately violated many recruiting rules based on what players, coaches, and athletic representatives told me, as well as other members of the investigating team.

My notes and those of other members of the investigating team, as well as the university's written statement of its position to the NCAA were voluminous. They were bound in large blue binders, which I held in my hands.

Cal called me as a witness in support of the university's defense. "Ms. Connell, would you please tell the jury what you discovered during your investigation of the alleged NCAA violations?"

I told the jury about our discovery of dozens of NCAA violations ranging from offers of cash to travel outside the thirty-mile boundary to recruits being taken to strip clubs in Memphis. I referred to my notes and reports, which I held in my lap.

"Your honor," Cal said, "I'd like to introduce Ms. Connell's notes and investigative reports into evidence."

Jim Waide stood

"Your honor, I object. Those notes are hearsay."

"The notes are not being introduced to prove that Coach Brewer or the university committed each wrongful act for which they are accused, but to prove that the university had a reasonable belief that Coach Brewer had willfully and deliberately violated NCAA rules," Cal argued. "Using the notes for that purpose *only* does not constitute hearsay."

It would be virtually impossible for the university to subpoena all the athletes, coaches, and athletic supporters who were interviewed across the country during the NCAA investigation.

"These notes and materials are what Ms. Connell and others on the investigative team *heard*," Judge Lackey said. "I want to hear it from the parties involved. The court finds the notes and reports to be hearsay. I'm not going to allow them to be entered into evidence."

My heart sank. The ruling was a huge blow to our case.

Even though my notes and materials were not admitted, Jim questioned me for hours about how the NCAA worked, how it investigated allegations of wrong-doing, details about each coach, student-athlete, and athletic booster had said, always framing his questions to make the NCAA look hard-hearted and as bad as possible. I answered each question honestly and with as much detail as I could provide to help the jury understand the rules and the evidence that the university had that Coach Brewer deliberately disregarded those rules.

"We do not have to belong to the NCAA," I explained, "but if we do, we are obligated to follow the rules."

This line of questioning went on so long that Judge Lackey finally called Cal and Jim to the bench and said to Jim: "Mr. Waide, I believe if I were you I would get this lady off the stand as fast as possible."

62

At the end of one day of the trial, Cal and university attorney Lee Tyner left the courtroom, drove to Hernando, and tried to convince Memphis businessman Steve Harris to come to Oxford to testify. Mr. Harris had been one of the persons named as participating in the infractions during the NCAA investigation which led to Coach Brewer's termination. Vice Chancellor Thomas Wallace encouraged Cal and Lee to pursue Mr. Harris as a witness. According to Dr. Wallace, Mr. Harris might just be willing to make amends for his wrongdoings by telling the truth at trial.

I was frustrated.

"You are wasting your time," I told them. "Steve Harris is never going to do that."

Mr. Harris had not admitted any violations to me or to our investigative team in the mid-1990s. I thought Cal and Lee were doing us all a disservice by trying to convince this man to testify.

"You should both be staying here at night preparing for trial," I admonished them.

I was wrong.

Cal and Lee did convince Mr. Harris to testify. I assumed he would tell them the same story he'd told me and the investigative team four years earlier.

On October 8, 1999, the Friday before Ole Miss played Tulane in Oxford at Vaught-Hemingway Stadium, Cal addressed the court.

"Your honor," Cal said, "The defense calls Steve Harris."

Jim Waide and Billy Brewer looked shocked. This witness was a complete surprise to them both.

Steve Harris, known affectionately among football boosters as "Big Steve," owned a boxing and packing company in Olive Branch and Southaven.

"Mr. Harris," Cal asked, "Tell us about the last time you saw Billy Brewer."

Mr. Harris said that Billy had come to his home a few weeks earlier. He testified that Coach Brewer had encouraged him to come to Oxford and tell the jury the same story he'd been telling the NCAA and our investigative team for years.

"Billy," Mr. Harris answered, "if they put me on the stand, under oath, I'm going to tell them the truth."

At that, according to Mr. Harris, Brewer stood and said, "Steve, I don't believe we need you to come to the trial."

"So, Mr. Harris," Cal asked, "why are you changing your story now?"

"I got tired of reading all the lies," he said. "There was no truth in what I told the NCAA or the university's representatives."

As the testimony went on, Mr. Harris told the jury that Billy Brewer did know about the recruits going to Memphis at Harris' expense — and that the Ole Miss recruiting coordinator had called him in advance to set up the trip.

"What did you do with the recruits?" Cal asked.

"They came to my home, watched some football on the big screen TV, then we went to a restaurant. I gave them some money to go out and have a good time."

"Did you take the recruits to a strip club?"

"No," Harris answered, "but they did go on their own."

"So, Mr. Harris," Cal asked, "why did you lie to the NCAA?"

"Billy was head coach, and his job was on the line."

"Did Coach Brewer know you were lying to the NCAA?" Cal asked.

"Four or five times, we talked about the investigation, and he told me to just keep denying everything. 'Just keep doing what you're doing.'"

When asked if Brewer knew about the recruits in question, the trip to Memphis, and the strip clubs, Mr. Harris answered, "We discussed it a day or two before."

Jim Waide stood.

"Your honor," he said, "we need to take a break."

Judge Lackey recessed the court. But he didn't leave the courtroom through the judge's chambers. Instead, Judge Lackey walked down the center aisle of the courtroom.

When he reached the railing that separates the lawyers from the audience, he pushed the swinging door open and said under his breath, "I believe the wheels just fell off the wagon."

63

Cal then put Warner Alford and Robert Khayat on the witness stand. It was particularly difficult for both men. Warner, Robert, and Billy had been teammates. Billy was the holder for Robert when he kicked field goals for Ole Miss. The two of them, along with the snapper, practiced together for hours after all the other teammates had finished. Billy and Robert were drafted the same year and were rookies together on the Washington Redskins team. Warner and Billy had worked together for nearly a decade as athletics director and head football coach.

Cal asked both men the same question: "Do you think the university was correct in firing Billy Brewer?"

Warner and Robert both answered "Yes."

The irony of all this — the culmination of two investigations, two NCAA probations, and this trial —is that it involved tension and disagreement among so many friends who had attended Ole Miss together and worked together at the university for years.

It hurt me to be a part of this pain — causing neighbors, former classmates, and friends to lose their jobs. It hurt me to see our university painted as a renegade school doing whatever it took to win at football.

As Warner and Robert took the stand to testify against their long-time friend Billy Brewer, I couldn't help but remember the first day I met them both as eager, hopeful, hungry freshmen with huge hands, taking the donuts I hoped to save for Dan Jordan.

In his closing arguments to the jury, Cal did a fantastic job defending the university's decision to terminate Coach Brewer. Like all good attorneys, he covered his bases.

"Even if you believe," he said, "Coach Brewer is due the amount remaining on his contract, that total would be $221,355, not the nearly $2M he is seeking."

64

The Brewer case went to the jury on October 12, 1999.

As the jury deliberated, I thought about the second NCAA investigation — which had cost the University of Mississippi millions of dollars in lost bowl and television revenue — as well as the damage this trial had inflicted. The deepest cost, perhaps, was the internal division between alumni who thought there was nothing wrong with breaking NCAA rules (*because everyone does it*) and those who thought the rules were made by our presidents, athletic directors, and coaches for a reason and should be followed.

I also knew there were critics who felt that if the university had been represented in this matter by a man, Ole Miss would not have received *any* sanctions by the NCAA.

The jury was out for just over an hour.

They filed back into the courtroom, and the jury foreman stood.

"Have you reached a decision?" Judge Lackey asked.

"We have, your honor. By a vote of 10-2, we find in favor of the plaintiff. We award Coach Brewer $221,355 in lost wages."

There was no award for emotional pain and suffering or punitive damages.

As I left the courtroom, I was met with cameras and television reporters. I was halfway down the stairs when a young woman put a microphone in front of my face.

"It looks like the university took a beating," she said. "What do you think about this?"

"I attended Ole Miss with Coach Brewer. I wish him well as he moves on with his life."

And I meant it. We were all friends once. What we needed now was rest. And time to heal.

No one left a winner.

65

While I was fighting public battles over Confederate symbols and the Billy Brewer suit, I continued to deal with private matters between individuals at the university.

Sexual harassment complaints, unfortunately, were far too common.

I was a bit more adept at handling the issues than I was the first time around when I threatened to humiliate a perpetrator in church.

Now, I understood the complexity of these accusations. Alleged harassers are almost considered guilty when a charge of harassment is filed. It takes wise, careful consideration to give fair treatment to both parties in these situations.

I experienced first-hand the harm that can befall an innocent person when wrongly accused of sexual harassment.

In 1999, a secretary in the office of a high-ranking university official made informal complaints of sexual harassment against him. Knowing the man well and working with him closely, I was certain these complaints had no merit and that something else was behind them.

I conducted the investigation myself and was meticulous in my thoroughness. After dozens of interviews with the complainant and witnesses she named, I found nothing to support her claims. I reported my findings to the chancellor and to the complainant. I advised her that she could take her complaint to the affirmative action/equal opportunity officer if she wished, but she should be aware that by making the accusations, whether she could prove them or not, she could ruin this man's career and subject herself to extensive questioning. She told me she would think about it overnight and inform me the next day of her decision.

Around 3:00 the following morning, my doorbell rang. I was frightened. When I opened the door, the woman — the complainant — was standing there. I saw a SUV in my drive with the motor running. Children were inside the vehicle. I invited her to come inside, and bring her children.

"No," she said, "I am running away from my abusive husband, and I need to leave now." Holding back tears, she said, "I came to tell you that I know you never believed any of the complaints I made. I want you to know that you were right. Everything I said was a lie. My husband forced me to make these false accusations."

She turned and walked toward her vehicle.

"I won't be making any more complaints. I'm getting as far away as I can from my husband."

66

In the early 2000s, I was in charge of raising money to buy a new organ for St. Peter's Episcopal Church in Oxford. I asked Chancellor Khayat to meet with me for an hour to discuss with me how to raise money. Although I was intimately involved in many aspects of the university, I was never involved directly in fundraising. The chancellor came to my office and told me that the secret to fundraising was to identify what the potential donor was interested in and then ask for financial support. I thanked him for his time and good advice.

He rose to leave, but stopped at the door and turned to me: "Sister, you need to return to law practice because as a fund-raiser you are no good at all."

I didn't understand.

"I have spent an hour with you," he said, "and you have not asked me for a dime."

"Chancellor," I countered, "whatever you give, I will match."

He stunned me with a generous contribution. I had no choice but to match his donation, which was more than I could afford, but he had called my bluff.

Most people knew about Chancellor Khayat's public battle over Confederate symbols. But behind the scenes he moved to remedy the other problems Dr. Foard and the Phi Beta Kappa headquarters had identified as obstacles.

He garnered gifts from generous donors: $8M to support the holdings of the John D. Williams Library; $5.4M to recreate the honors program as the Sally McDonnell Barksdale Honors College; a $60M equivalency gift to create the Croft Institute for International Studies; $30M from two former law students as an endowment for faculty salaries; and a $25M commitment from the Gertrude C. Ford Foundation for a state-of-the-art performing arts center.

The University of Mississippi Foundation undertook the responsibilities for conducting a campaign for the private support that would fund academic enrichment projects for the library, scholarships, faculty salaries, and the honors program. The Phil Hardin Foundation provided a $24,000 grant to support the work of the Phi Beta Kappa application committee and subsequently gave a $450,000 grant to the university to be used in pursuit of a Phi Beta Kappa chapter.

With the endorsement of the Phi Beta Kappa faculty, Chancellor Khayat asked Dr. Ronald Schroeder, associate professor of English and a Phi Beta Kappa graduate of Wesleyan University, to serve as chair of the application committee and offered the logistical support of the Office of the University Attorney to compile the massive amount of data required for the application. Dr. Schroeder and I met in my office to begin discussions of how to organize and allow this project to begin.

The first question Dr. Schroeder asked me was: "Do you use the serial comma?"

"Yes, I do," I told him.

"What a relief," he exclaimed. "Now I know that we can work together."

Dr. Schroeder is a perfectionist. His meticulous attention to detail with both the data and the writing resulted in a well-received 108-page preliminary application and, subsequently, in a much longer and more complicated general report that contained detailed information regarding virtually every facet of the university's mission and operation. The collaborative work in compiling this latter document required an entire year.

On September 30, 1998, Dr. Schroeder delivered the 418-page general report to the Phi Beta Kappa committee on qualifications, which gave its approval of the written application. Shortly thereafter, a team of visitors from Phi Beta Kappa came to visit the campus. Over three days, they conducted an extensive study of the university's resources that supported the application. Impressed with all they saw, the site team made a positive recommendation to the committee on qualifications, which approved and recommended to the Phi Beta Kappa senate that the faculty at the University of Mississippi shelter a chapter. The senate adopted the affirmative recommendation of the committee and sent its positive vote to the society's council.

The final step in the process came on October 21, 2000, when Phi Beta Kappa council delegates from all over the nation voted "overwhelmingly in favor" of establishing a Phi Beta Kappa chapter at the University of Mississippi. Within minutes, accolades and congratulations poured in from faculty, students, alumni, donors, and officials at other universities.

Dr. Foard praised the chancellor: "Give Khayat the credit," he said. "He has brought the university to Phi Beta Kappa standards in all the areas identified in the past as weaknesses."

On the day of the Ole Miss Homecoming football game against UNLV on October 28, 2000, a plane flew over Vaught-Hemingway Stadium towing a banner that said: "Phi Beta Kappa Comes to Ole Miss."

Joy, pride, and celebration over this achievement permeated the air on Homecoming Day, rivaling the excitement over Ole Miss' 43-40 win in overtime. Warner Alford, former athletics director, described the occasion: "It was like winning the national championship."

Jesse Phillips, publisher of *The Oxford Eagle*, described the occasion as "Ole Miss scores academic 'touchdown.'" Mr. Phillips went on to say: "None of the university's great moments; i.e., a national championship in football, going to the College World Series in baseball or competing in post-season play of basketball, tennis or golf, equal The University of Mississippi being tapped by Phi Beta Kappa."

On April 6, 2001, the university held a formal ceremony in the Circle in front of the historic Lyceum Building to celebrate the University of Mississippi becoming the first chapter of Phi Beta Kappa at a public university in Mississippi. (Millsaps College sheltered the first chapter in Mississippi in 1988.) Dogwoods and redbuds were bursting into bloom on this cool spring day as Dr. Joseph W. Gordon of Yale University, national president of the Phi Beta Kappa Society, installed the Beta of Mississippi chapter in

Ole Miss celebrates its Phi Beta Kappa chapter

an afternoon ceremony. Dr. Niall Slater of Emory University, vice president of the society, delivered an address after initiation of fifty-six students from the top ten percent of those in the College of Liberal Arts were given the Golden Key of Phi Beta Kappa.

Dr. Schroeder commented after the ceremony: "Our pursuit of a chapter of Phi Beta Kappa for The University of Mississippi involved a partnership between faculty, students, administrators, staff, alumni and friends, the likes of which I have never seen before. I think I speak for my colleagues when I thank Chancellor Khayat for making our initiative the focal point of his administration and for marshaling people's support of the academic mission of the university."

Chancellor Khayat responded: "I am excited for our community and for the students who will be inducted and their families. All of us are grateful to Dr. Schroeder and the members of Phi Beta Kappa for bringing this prestigious organization to our campus."

67

One of the highlights of Chancellor Khayat's administration was the building of the Paris-Yates Chapel and Peddle Bell Tower in the area between the John D. Williams Library and Guyton Hall, the old medical school building. When discussions first began about reviving interest in building a chapel on state-owned land, questions arose as to whether this could be legally done. While donors Henry and Lee Paris were negotiating successfully with the American Civil Liberties Union (ACLU) and receiving a letter promising that no ACLU funds would ever be used to remove the Paris family symbol from the chapel, I was working with the head of the Mississippi ACLU to be sure that the university built the chapel and formulated use policies that would be consistent with the civil liberties ACLU was dedicated to protecting. Long hours of discussion took place between the head of ACLU in Mississippi and me concerning the legalities of what we as a public university could and could not do. Discussions running parallel with those the Parises were having ended with an agreement that any such chapel would not only be non-denominational, but would also be open to all faiths, whether Christian, Jewish, Muslim, Buddhist, Hindu, or people of no faith.

With commitments of $500,000 each from the Paris and Yates families for the chapel, and the Peddle family for the bell tower, Chancellor Khayat asked Don Frugé and the University of Mississippi Foundation to assume responsibility for building and paying for the chapel. Don and the Foundation worked together to raise the $3.8 million necessary to make the dream of the chapel a reality. Don and his wife, Mary Ann, co-chaired planning the dedication service, which was held on April 28, 2001.

The highlight of the service came as Mary Ann Frugé spoke and explained that every religious organization on campus was represented at the ceremony. She then asked each of the representatives to stand and articulate in one word what the chapel would mean to his or her organization. There were over 20 student religious organizations represented. Mary Ann asked them one by one to proceed to the bell tower and speak the one word chosen by their group. She directed them that when the last person spoke, all would join hands as a symbol of the unity of purpose as reflected in one's faith and, concurrently, as a symbol of the beauty of diversity. Many representatives of eastern religions wore their traditional religious attire. I stood in awe at the diversity of faith, clothing, religious garb, and nationalities united in love and peace. As the students from all walks of life uttered their one, carefully selected word and joined around the bell tower hand in hand, the University of Mississippi Concert Singers performed a moving rendition of *What a Wonderful World*.

The Paris-Yates Chapel is a widely used building on campus, hosting weddings, church services, organizational meetings of both people of faith and those not sharing the same faith.

68

Throughout my association with Chancellor Khayat as a friend, a professional colleague, and my university's chancellor, I have observed him to be a caring and charismatic person.

Chancellor Khayat implemented many changes that improved morale and the quality of life for faculty, staff, and students. He rescheduled sorority and fraternity recruitment from the first week of school to the second month of the fall semester, which allowed new students to meet their classes for a month or so, receive six-weeks grade reports, learn their way around the campus, and adjust to college life before the distraction and pressure of recruitment began. He directed that the library be open 24 hours a day, signifying to students that the university's central educational facility was available to them at all times. He endorsed the work of a task force appointed to examine the university's academic program and to formulate a core curriculum that was required of all lower-division students. He directed that more Friday afternoon classes be scheduled, which resulted in more students staying on the campus

In my opinion, he is a true "Renaissance Man." He has studied history and literature, read and written poetry, appreciated music and the arts, and engaged in the life of the university community in all its multi-faceted layers.

He is the embodiment of what the liberal arts and higher education are about.

He also engages in an almost lost art — the art of letter writing. He has written, in his identifiable penmanship, thousands of notes and letters to friends, supporters, and even enemies of the university.

I have been the beneficiary of a number of his notes and letters, which I treasure. In each one, he took the time to single me out for a compliment with words that were personal and meaningful to me. I especially treasure notes he wrote during the trying days of the NCAA investigations and

Brewer trial; those thanking me for nominating him as the Oxford-University-Lafayette County "Citizen of the Year" in 1988; thanking me for attending Robert, Jr.'s wedding in Princeton, New Jersey, in May 2002, and numerous other occasions. He always wrote with both kindness and a sense of humor.

He once wrote thanking me for making the Khayat family a pound cake on the occasion of a visit by their daughter Margaret and her husband David, in which he wrote, "You need a patent on your pound cake. I don't know if you learned how to cook in Louisville, the Delta, or Oxford, but we are so glad you did."

Chancellor Khayat was a strong supporter of women's athletics, of the leadership efforts of Senior Woman Administrator Lynnette Johnson, in support of gender equity in athletics, and has taken pride in the large number of women superstars Ole Miss has fielded: Jennifer and Peggie Gillom, and Armintie Price in women's basketball; Poloma Collantes in women's tennis; Brittany Reese, our Olympian long jumper; and Coach Van Chancellor in coaching of women's basketball.

Peggie still holds the school's record for scoring and rebounding, while Jennifer was an Olympic medalist, Kodak All-American, and SEC Female Athlete of the Year. Coach Chancellor built his legacy with 18 years as the Lady Rebels' coach, where he compiled a record of 439 wins and 154 losses and has been ranked in the top 20 nation-wide for the all-time winning coaches of a women's basketball team. Peggie, Jennifer and Van are all inducted into the WBB Hall of Fame. Coach Chancellor is also a member of the Naismith Basketball Hall of Fame, which is the highest honor in women's basketball. Price was named to the All-SEC First Team three times and became the first player to be named two-time SEC Defensive Player of the Year.

Under Chancellor Khayat's leadership and through the generosity of donors he solicited on behalf of women's opportunities in athletics, Ole

Miss has engaged in two building projects that have added much to its commitment to gender equity. The first was the building of the Women's Athletics Complex in 1997 and the naming and dedication of that facility to Jennifer and Peggie Gillom in 2000. The second is the dedication in 2013 of the Manning Center for the benefit of both women and men student-athletes.

As I began considering retirement, I hosted a luncheon at my home and invited Carol Ross, the coach of women's basketball; Lynnette Johnson; Peggie Gillom; Kat King; Margaret King; Diann Coleman; Margaret Sims; and Mary Sharp Rayner, president of the Ole Miss Alumni Association. We had a delightful time talking and laughing and eating together. I love to cook and think I am a fairly good cook. It matters to me what people think of my cooking. During the course of dining, we talked about foods we like and disliked.

"I cannot stand squash, and my Mama is always cooking it," Peggie said.

The conversation moved on until Peggie spoke again, saying "Ms. Connell, what is this casserole? I really like it."

"Peggie," I replied, "I hate to ruin it for you, but it is a squash casserole."

We all laughed and acknowledge that if you cover something with enough cheese and sauce, you can make even the serious doubters give praise.

During the spring semester of 2003, I began preparation for retirement from the university attorney position. I thought it was time to pass the torch to a younger and well-qualified generation. When I announced my retirement, the university hosted a reception for me at Memory House, the former home of John Faulkner, William Faulkner's brother, and the following day in the Lyceum. I was honored by how many people attended the events, and I treasure the photographs I have of them. These people were my family. I knew I was going to miss them and the daily involvement in the life of the university, and I still do. I never walk back into the Lyceum, or any place on the campus of the university, without a longing for those days again.

Lee Tyner, Mary Ann, Susan Tyner, and
Chancellor Robert Khayat at the Connell retirement reception

X
Mayo Mallette

69

In April of 2003, shortly before I retired from the university, Cal Mayo and Pope Mallette invited me to lunch at the Downtown Grill on the Oxford Square.

We met outside under the restaurant's balcony, walked into the Grill, and were escorted to a table under the stairs. The three of us made small talk for a few minutes before Cal leaned forward and put his hands on the table.

"What are you planning to do?" he asked.

Several weeks before, I was randomly seated next to a gentleman on an airline flight. We struck up a conversation, and I mentioned that I would soon be retiring as university attorney at Ole Miss.

"What are you going to do?" he asked.

It seemed to be everybody's question.

"I don't know," I told him. "I'm going to explore opportunities."

"Have you thought about teaching?" he asked.

"I've taught forever," I said, smiling. "Yes, I'd be very interested in teaching."

"We have a program at Seton Hall we're trying to develop," he told me. "It's a higher education law program. You sound like the perfect person to get involved with this program. Why don't you come up and interview for the position?"

I had always dreamed of living in New York City. In fact, I had tried to work and live in the city as a young woman before I moved to California. Now, opportunity to live in New York had again presented itself.

I used the interview as an excuse to visit the city again.

I took the train out to Seton Hall in South Orange, New Jersey, about forty-five minutes outside the city. The visit to the university was wonderful; I loved the campus, the people, and, of course, the opportunity. But when it was time for me to go back to the city, I walked to the train station in the dark. I was alone in South Orange.

The station was in an isolated area, and it was dark. I waited on the platform for the train, hoping I had read the signs correctly and was waiting for the right train. I started to feel anxious and vulnerable in this unfamiliar place, isolated in the darkness.

The train finally arrived and, as it turned out, it was the correct one. But after the forty-five-minute ride back into the city, I realized I had to find my way back to the hotel.

This was a taste, I knew, of the realities of commuting every day in New York. I was beginning to have second thoughts.

I looked up at Cal, who still had his hands on the table.

"I'm going to live in New York," I said. "I have an opportunity to teach at Seton Hall."

"Are you sure you really want to leave the South, leave your roots, and live that far away?" Cal asked me.

I could not help but think about what my daughter Stella had told me when I started planning to move to New York. She had lived in the city for ten years at that point, and she planted my dreams in reality. She said I could not afford to live in New York with the lifestyle I wanted.

"You don't want to live in New York," she had told me flatly over the phone. "You love coming to New York to attend plays, the opera, symphonies, and dine at fine restaurants. When you live here, you don't do those things on a daily basis. You go to work, go out on occasion with friends, attend cultural events sometimes, but you do not live the way visitors to New York do. It's not the world you know."

I was still considering all of this when Pope spoke up.

"We want to expand our education law practice," he said. "We think you could help do that. We would like to have you join us in an 'of counsel' role."

I would not be an associate, and I would certainly not be a partner. But I would be allowing the firm to use my reputation to promote their business, and I would be acting as a rainmaker helping to get business for the firm.

70

Within a few weeks, I accepted the offer to work at Mayo Mallette.

Early on during my tenure at Mayo Mallette, Cal asked me to write a proposal to the IHL board asking them to provide funding for us to travel to the various state universities and present employment law seminars. I spent a lot of time writing the proposal, and I spent hours on the phone with college presidents, academic vice presidents, university attorneys, and human resource directors trying to get Mayo Mallette's name ingrained as a place to turn for advice on higher education issues.

Cal, Pope, and I spent a lot of time traveling to the seven Mississippi public universities.

One night, we stayed in Vicksburg at Annabelle Bed and Breakfast, a beautiful antebellum home with three stories, no elevator, and narrow stairs. The men had a challenging time getting my too-full suitcase up to the third floor.

The next day, we visited Alcorn State University to give a seminar. I had never visited that beautiful campus before. When I got out of the car on campus, all I could think was, "This is where Ruby Dee spent four years of her life."

We gave seminars on higher education law.

I called my colleagues at other universities.

I wrote thank you notes.

I talked on the phone.

I went to lunch with friends.

This was all enjoyable, but I missed being on campus and doing real legal work.

Cal was representing Alcorn State University at that time in a complicated case involving a group of thugs who had clandestinely entered the Alcorn campus, killed one student, and injured another.

I watched Cal working hard on the case, and I thought, "That's what I want to do."

I had exhausted my budget, as well as my taste, for taking friends out to lunch on the Square. I was itching for some real legal work.

One day, I walked into Cal's office and asked if he had a moment. He invited me to sit down.

"Cal, do you have anything I can do on this case?" I asked.

"Oh yes, I need some help!" he said.

We worked very well together. I traveled to Alcorn and interviewed witnesses. Sometimes Cal accompanied me. Other times, he went alone. After a few weeks, he came into my office.

"I want to move for summary judgment," he said.

This meant that if we were successful, the judge would dismiss the case altogether. I assisted in writing the brief. Cal argued the summary judgment motion before Judge Pickard, who dismissed the motion.

The case proceeded to a bench trial (a trial before a judge without a jury) before Judge Pickard, who ruled in the university's favor.

The plaintiffs appealed.

I assisted in writing the brief to the Mississippi Supreme Court, arguing that the wrongful acts in question (the shooting of the deceased and injured students) were not caused by any negligence of Alcorn, but by the wrongful acts of a third party that were intervening, superseding, causes of the injuries that relieved Alcorn of any legal liability.

I relied heavily on Professor Bob Weems' treatise *Mississippi Law of Torts* in writing my part of the brief, arguing that the university was not legally liable for the intervening wrongful acts of a third party (the shooter). Both Judge Pickard and the Mississippi Supreme Court relied heavily on Professor Weems' book in deciding for Alcorn and ruling in favor of the university.

71

We represented Delta State University in a sex discrimination and retaliation suit filed by a man who did not receive an administrative position. He claimed that a younger woman obtained the position because she was having an affair with a high-level university administrator. Both the woman and the university denied that an affair took place.

The university maintained that the woman was better qualified and moved for summary judgment on the sex discrimination claim, which the district court granted. The plaintiff further claimed that the university retaliated against him for complaining to the university's president that the woman was selected only because of her relationship with one of the vice presidents, which, he contended, constituted "paramour favoritism" in violation of Title VII (the section of the Civil Rights Act of 1964 that prohibits discrimination in employment on the basis of race, sex, national origin, or religion).

I asked Paul Watkins, our Mayo Mallette law clerk at the time and who was number one in his law school class, to research the issue of *paramour favoritism* and whether it violated Title VII.

Paul looked at me with a blank expression.

"What is a 'paramour?'" he asked.

"A 'paramour' is one's lover," I explained.

"I've got it," he said hastily. "You want to know if it is illegal to show favoritism in employment to someone with whom you're having an affair."

"That's right," I said.

As it turned out, paramour favoritism, while highly immoral, was not illegal under Title VII. Cal argued the case before an alert and interested Judge Biggers, who engaged in a spirited discourse with Cal over the legal issue. The judge pressed Cal and argued the other side, but Cal stood his ground and in the end, the judge agreed.

"You know, you're right," he said. "It may not be fair, and it may not be right, but it's not illegal."

We handled litigation matters for all the public universities through the years, ranging from suits based on allegations of discrimination in hiring, wrongful termination, tenure denial, and various tort claims. One of the most interesting cases arose from the grade appeal of a student who sued not only the University of Mississippi but also four of his professors in their individual capacities for giving him grades with which he disagreed and accusing him of plagiarism and academic dishonesty.

In that case a student asked her professor if she could speak with him privately after she turned her paper in. "Professor," she said, "I have been watching a fellow student and have seen him take the notes out on several occasions, look at them, and then write answers to exam questions. I think he is cheating, which is unfair to those of us who have studied hard and relied on what we have learned in answering the questions."

"Thank you," the professor responded. "I will watch him more closely."

The professor began to watch the student carefully and observed the same thing.

When the student turned his exam paper in, the professor said: "I would like for you to show me the notes you have inside your jacket that you have been consulting during this exam."

After first denying that he had any concealed notes, the student finally handed the notes to the professor and said, "But this is not cheating because these notes did not help me at all."

As to the plagiarism charge, the student argued: "Even though I copied much of the paper of another, I did mention his name at one point in the paper so I have not plagiarized."

The professor disagreed and gave the student an "F". The student sued.

The university and each of the sued faculty members moved for summary judgment, which Judge Aycock granted all defendants.

During my time at Mayo Mallette, I tried several *pro se* cases. Parties representing themselves without the assistance of an attorney are known as *pro se* litigants. *Pro se* is Latin for "in one's own behalf."

The most persistent and tenacious *pro se* litigant I faced was a gentleman named Lester Washington. He stood 6' 3". He was a middle-aged man who had a number of conflicts with Jackson State University.

Mr. Washington filed a series of actions against the university that endured for nearly a decade. He sued dozens of individuals and entities, including the Fifth Circuit Court of Appeals. Mr. Washington would frequently copy Supreme Court justices on his rambling pleadings.

In one action, Mr. Washington contended that after he was dismissed from the university's clinical psychology program for academic reasons, he was subsequently refused re-admission because he had earlier filed a charge of discrimination against the university with EEOC.

Jackson State University is a historically black institution. The defendant named in the case was black. Mr. Washington was black.

The university defended its decision not to readmit him to the clinical psychology doctoral program because he ranked twenty-ninth out of twenty-nine applicants. He failed to show that he was treated differently from any other applicant of a different race to support his discrimination claim under Title VI of the Civil Rights Act of 1964. He failed to show that he was an employee of the university able to invoke the protections of Title VII of the Civil Rights Act. Accordingly, U.S. District Court Judge Dan Jordan, in a beautifully written, twenty-three-page opinion, dismissed the claims.

Judge Jordan is the son of Dr. Dan Jordan, Jr., former head of the Thomas Jefferson Foundation (Monticello), "Scholar in Residence" at the University of Virginia, and the boy I tried to impress at the Methodist Church as a sophomore when Mary Ann Mobley and I passed out donuts. Judge Jordan had also been a student of mine at Ole Miss. I had taught him business law.

I'd been nervous about submitting a brief to a former student. It was obvious that he was not equally nervous, because Judge Jordan wrote a superior opinion — one that far exceeded my brief. It is an opinion to which all university attorneys now refer when addressing similar Title VI and Title VII issues.

In another of Mr. Washington's *pro se* cases, I had a hearing before U.S. District Judge Henry Wingate in Jackson, Mississippi. In the middle of our motion hearing, around 5:30 p.m., Judge Wingate stopped the hearing.

"I have to go teach a class at Mississippi College Law School," he told us. "We'll reconvene at 7:30 p.m. after my class is over."

I had over two hours on my hands before Judge Wingate would resume the hearing.

I walked down Capitol Street to the Walthall Hotel coffee shop and waited there until it was time to return to the courthouse. It was winter, and while I was waiting, the sun had gone down.

At 7:30 p.m., I walked back up Capitol Street to the courthouse, but when I arrived at the federal building, I found that the front door was locked. There was no marshal around to let me in. The only light came from the line of shops across the street.

I was cold. I stood in my black business suit, in the dark, waiting, holding my briefcase and purse. I was aware of how vulnerable I was in downtown Jackson. I tucked my purse under my arm.

As I stood waiting, I noticed a group of men roaming the street. They were young and shabbily dressed. There were easily a dozen of them, and a few of them began to look my way. I grew more and more uneasy as they circled.

"Hey," I heard one of the men say, "over there," nodding in my direction.

I did not know what to do. I did not want to show how nervous I was, and I certainly did not want to take off running. I looked across the street at

St. Andrews Episcopal Cathedral. It was dark, abandoned. As was the Governor's mansion adjacent to the courthouse. I hoped a police officer would turn the corner, but none did.

Just then, one of the men started up the steps towards me. I couldn't see his face under his hood.

"Gimme your purse," he said.

I had no way to defend myself against him, or the other men behind him. My heart was pounding. I was about to toss my purse on the ground when a huge figure stepped out of the darkness behind me.

"Get out of here," he said, in a loud, commanding voice. "Leave her alone."

It was Mr. Washington, our *pro se* plaintiff.

The would-be thief stepped back and retreated down the steps. The rest of the men melted away into the darkness.

"Thank you," I said, turning to Mr. Washington.

I was so grateful he was there, willing to help, even though we were opponents in court.

We waited about ten more minutes, before a marshal came to let us in, and we reconvened the hearing.

The motion argument went on late into the night. Mr. Washington was getting irritable. He began arguing with the judge.

"You don't know what you're talking about," Mr. Washington told Judge Wingate.

"You stop right now," Judge Wingate said to Mr. Washington, "and look over your shoulder at the window up on the second floor overlooking the courtroom. Behind that window sits a United States Marshal with a gun. A big gun. If you are disrespectful to me one more time, I am going to give him a signal and he is going to come through these courtroom doors with his gun and put you in jail."

At that moment, the door to the courtroom opened, and the marshal, who looked like John Wayne, walked in. He took a seat in the jury box close to the plaintiff, who immediately stopped arguing with the judge.

I also defended Jackson State University in a religious discrimination case by another *pro se* plaintiff. He sued the university for terminating him. The plaintiff refused to work the midnight shift as a residence hall receptionist. He maintained that because he was Muslim, he needed to study the Koran and pray between 2:00 a.m. and 4:00 a.m.

He argued that to require him to work the midnight shift was discrimination against him on the basis of his religion.

The university showed that it gave him time off to pray during his work hours and that all residence hall receptionists had taken turns working the night shift. It would have been unduly burdensome for Jackson State to arrange for other employees to cover the plaintiff's assigned midnight shifts, possibly incur overtime expenses, and cause other employees to assume a disproportionate workload, all of which would pose an undue hardship as a matter of law on the university and was not required by Title VII.

Jackson State further showed that plaintiff's immediate supervisor, who recommended his termination, was also Muslim, which further weakened his religious discrimination claim.

In working on this case, I read the Koran.

I particularly focused on the footnote that addressed the preference for praying at night when one is not distracted by the work of the day.

I became interested in furthering my knowledge of Islam and took a course taught by a University of Mississippi professor, Dr. Mary Thurlkill, associate professor of philosophy and religion, which was sponsored by the Oxford Newcomer's Club.

The course attracted a number of attendees. Dr. Thurlkill was an excellent, highly energized teacher. The class was capped at fifty. Each week ten to fifteen people waited in line to see if someone who had signed up for the class failed to appear, thereby freeing a space for one or more standing in line. We visited the local mosque where the imam explained the Muslim prayer service.

The Mayo Mallette Team

We were then invited to a table laden with sweets and enjoyed fellowship with nearly two dozen of our local Muslim faculty and students.

In the meantime, Jackson State University moved for summary judgment in the religious discrimination case, which Judge Lee granted.

72

The Browning Club of Oxford was formed in 1895 and named for Elizabeth Barrett Browning. Its purpose was to provide an outlet for women who enjoyed reading and discussing literature with friends in the homes of members.

On March 4, 1969, I gave a program to the club on "The Peabody Hotel," the subject of my master's thesis in history. We met in the home of Madge Stubblefield on Country Club Road. All of the members were lovely to me. Having no family in Oxford and little opportunity to meet and mix with older members of the Oxford community, I had a delightful time in this diverse, multi-generational mix of women.

Bill asked when I returned home, "How was the Browning Club?"

"Wonderful," I exclaimed. "I felt that I belonged to a real community such as I had in Louisville and Clarksdale."

How I hoped that someday I might be a member of such an interesting group of women. Little did I know then that my wish would soon come true or that 1969 would be such a special year in my life.

First, our third daughter, Mary Ann, was born on September 14, the same day as my grandparents' wedding anniversary and my father's birthday.

Next, on October 14, 1969, the Browning Club invited Laura Bradley and me to attend the club as guests. Two weeks later, the club extended an invitation to Laura and me to join the club. We were thrilled.

"Laura, how do we respond? By letter or a phone call?"

"By letter and on our nicest stationery," Laura said. "Also," she said, "we need to say we accept 'with pleasure'".

We both accepted with pleasure the invitation and began to be a part of this remarkable group of women. Like those who had gone before us, we washed our windows, polished our silver, and agonized over what to serve when it came our turn to hostess the club in our home. I recall that we spent a considerable amount of time deciding if we should serve salted pecans or cheese straws or both.

When hostessing, we always had our children dressed in their finest to make a brief appearance at the club meeting. They were then carried away by a babysitter or housekeeper so as not to interfere with the business and program of the club. I recall Thera Jones, a lovely woman who worked with me for a number of years, bringing my daughter Stella (age two) into the living room of our home on Phillip Road for her brief appearance. Stella did not disappoint. Before Thera whisked her away, she smiled and laughed and looked beautiful in a lovely Lillian Shop dress her grandmother had given her.

Programs through the years have been interesting, intellectual, and diverse. We have had outstanding presenters ranging from Dr. Charles Eagles speaking on his book, *The Price of Defiance*; world-renowned concert pianist Bruce Levingston performing works by Phillip Glass that he would soon be playing in Carnegie Hall; to Tucker Carrington speaking on The Innocence Project, a program sponsored in part by John Grisham to provide legal representation to prisoners who have been wrongfully convicted and incarcerated for crimes they did not commit.

While the club does entertain with graciousness and pays due respect to the array of speakers, it is not without its lighter moments.

At the May 4, 1993, meeting in the home of Mary Ann Frugé, architect Tom Howorth was speaking to the club on local architecture and the restoration of Barnard Observatory, a historic building on campus. After about 15 minutes, Madge Stubblefield put up her hand to speak.

"Tom," she said, "we have heard enough of this. What we really want you to talk about are which houses in Oxford you think are really tacky!"

During the years when I served as university attorney, I found it difficult to attend the meetings because they were held in the middle of the workday. Several times I submitted my letter of resignation because of the difficulty I had in always being present. Mrs. Beanland would not hear of it and told me each time I discussed with her my feelings of guilt that I could not always be present, "Go ahead and submit your letter of resignation, but I will see that it is rejected." So I remained active, serving as president three times and on the program committee six times.

It is hard to explain the Browning Club to people from other parts of the country. On one occasion, we were trying to find a date for a NACUA conference call. Tuesday afternoon at 3:00 was proposed.

I immediately responded, "No, that will not work for me because I have Browning Club then."

One of my colleagues from California asked, "What in the world is the Browning Club that meets in the middle of the work day?"

I explained, "It is a ladies' literary club that means a great deal to me and keeps me rooted in a world of graciousness and civility and contact with women of all ages who are smart, interesting, kind, and loyal to each other. Living in a town with no relatives, it is like an extended family to me."

"It sounds like *Gone with the Wind* to me," she exclaimed.

"Perhaps it is in some ways, but in the good ways where dignity and graciousness prevail."

Each meeting of the Browning Club begins with a collect, which was written by Mary Stuart in 1904 and is used by women's clubs in Canada, the United States, Britain, and other countries. My daughter Stella prepared a lovely calligraphy inscription of the prayer, had it framed, and gave it to me for Christmas one year. I hang it in my den with pride and gratefulness that this part of the past has been such a meaningful part of my life.

The Browning Club Prayer

Keep us, Oh God, from pettiness;
let us be large in thought, in word, in deed.

Let us be done with fault-finding
and leave off self-seeking.

May we put away all pretense and meet each
other face to face – without self-pity
and without prejudice.

May we never be hasty in judgment and
always generous.

Let us take time for all things;
make us to grow calm, serene, gentle.

Teach us to put into action our better impulses,
straightforward and unafraid.

Grant that we may realize it is the little
things that create differences,
that in the big things of life we are at one.

And may we strive to touch and to know the great,
common human heart of us all, and
O Lord God, let us forget not to be kind!

Mary Stuart

73

In 2003, John Samonds, an associate dean at the UM Honors College and a leader at St. Peter's Episcopal Church, asked if he could put my name forward as a candidate for the vestry. I told him I was honored and added that I finally had time to serve. The election was held at the annual parish meeting in January 2004. I was elected to serve my first of three terms as a vestry member.

During those years, we had a number of legal issues arise at St. Peter's, which I was able to handle, including the purchase of a neighboring house; termination of a trust left to the church by a former parishioner (so the church could receive and manage the proceeds without having to pay large corporate fees to a Birmingham bank); fight a claim by an adjoining landowner that a church easement was his property; and negotiate with AT&T over their cable lines on church property.

Through the years as I served on the vestry — and especially when performing legal work for the church — I smiled when I remembered the call The Rev. Don Morse made to Bill all those years ago to ask if I could serve on the vestry.

Somehow I think Bill would give a different answer if he were alive today.

In the fall of 2003, Guy Gillespie resigned as attorney for the Oxford School District. The district advertised the position, conducted a search for his successor, and I applied.

On December 22, 2003, the school board selected me as the attorney for the school district.

During my time as school board attorney, Dr. Kim Stasny became the district superintendent and led the school district to the successful passage of a $30 million bond issue to build a new high school and perform restorative work on other school buildings. Significant time and work were involved in acquiring the land, working with the architect, and contractor, Yates Construction. A beautiful new Oxford High School and renovations of other facilities resulted.

Unfortunately, Dr. Stasny developed a brain tumor and died before the new high school was completed. She made a lasting contribution to the Oxford School District with her innovative ideas, energy, commitment to excellence in education, and loving personality. I was pleased to see the school board choose Brian Harvey, my daughter Jane's childhood "Big Wheels" friend from across the street, to serve first as interim superintendent and then as the permanent one. I enjoyed working with Brian as well as with the outstanding members of the Oxford School Board and thought they did, and continue to do, a fine job.

While serving as the board attorney, I attended all the state-wide meetings of the Council of School Board attorneys and eventually was elected president of the organization. Through association with other school board attorneys, I learned much and always had someone to call to ask for help instead of having to reinvent the wheel at every turn. We were served well by Mike Waldrop and the Mississippi Association of School Boards.

In May 2011, I resigned as attorney for the Oxford School District. Paul Watkins was ready to step in and take over representation of the district in a superior way, so it seemed the right time to step away from that work. Marian Barksdale wrote me a lovely note of appreciation of my work. I miss the work and the personal friendships and associations. I miss being a part of the discussions of what is going on in our city school system.

I will always be grateful that I had the opportunity to be involved with the Oxford School District.

Even after I retired as university attorney, I continued to remain active in NACUA, speaking frequently at the Lawyers New to Higher Education Conference immediately preceding the annual conference, serving on the editorial board of *The Journal of College and University Law*, publishing articles in the Journal, and attending annual conferences. In June 2002, NACUA honored me with the Distinguished Service Award at the annual conference in Boston.

Through the years, numerous NACUA colleagues have given me support, guidance, and friendship as I have dealt with legal issues affecting higher education institutions. I have never called a NACUA colleague for help who has not returned my call, nor have I ever asked for advice or assistance that was not given by a member of the association.

All NACUA attorneys agree that there is not another professional association like it. Because universities are not in adversarial relationships with each other (except on the playing fields of athletics), NACUA attorneys believe, as I do, that what is good for one university is good for all higher education institutions. Through the collegiality and leadership of NACUA, higher education is made stronger.

Reflecting back over my years of involvement with NACUA, several experiences and relationships stand out: my friendship with Chris Helwick, when she was general counsel for California State University, who helped me understand the challenges large, multi-campus institutions face; Pam Bernard, general counsel for both the University of Florida and then Duke University, who encouraged me to become actively involved in NACUA; and, Barbara Lee, professor and associate provost at Rutgers University and the world's leading scholar and writer on higher education legal issues, who mentored me both personally and professionally, especially on the subject of collegiality in higher education employment decisions, a subject upon which she spoke at the Stetson Conference on Law and Higher Education in 1984.

In 2001, I was part of a search committee to find a new chief executive officer for NACUA. One of my assignments was to contact the applicants' references. When I called those people listed by Kathleen Santora, I heard glowing reviews that made all others pale by comparison. She immediately moved to the top of the list.

When we called her in for interviews, we became even more impressed. Over the course of her previous career, she had been a member of NACUA and understood the association. She displayed intelligence, grace, personality, and warmth.

Kathleen was the right person for the position. On the evening before Kathleen's first day on the job, I called her at her home.

"I wish you well," I told her. "We're so pleased to have you as our CEO."

"Oh, thank you!" she said, sounding taken aback. "I so appreciate your calling."

The 2014 NACUA conference was scheduled to be held in Denver.

I had never had an allergy in my life, but several days before the conference I developed a severe sinus infection and painful ear aches.

I finally went to see Dr. Ford Dye, my ENT doctor.

"Ms. Connell," he said, "your ears are terribly infected. I suspect from an allergy that caused your sinus infection."

"Then, Dr. Dye, you need to prescribe something that will work fast because I am going to the NACUA conference in Denver in a few days, and I am speaking there."

"You're not speaking anywhere," Dr. Dye said, "because you are not going to a conference in Denver with these ears."

"I have to go," I protested, determined not to miss a fourth NACUA conference in my thirty-two years of involvement with the association.

I left his office unhappy and frustrated, determined to seek another opinion. I went to see my pharmacist and friend, Bill McClellan at G & M Pharmacy. Surely, I thought, he would be able to give me something to knock out the infection.

"You want to get on a plane and go to Denver with your ears?" he asked incredulously when I told him my situation. "Look," he said, "I've had severe ear infections, and I know what that pain is like. I'm telling you that if you go with this infection, when you get off that plane and the Denver altitude hits your ears, you won't make it ten feet before falling out. I'm not giving you anything because you are not going to Denver."

I was devastated. I left his pharmacy and the next morning called Barbara Lee, with whom I was scheduled to speak.

"Barbara," I said with consternation, "I cannot come to the conference. I have an earache."

"I imagine it's a lot more than an earache or you would be coming," she said. "But, do not worry; we will miss you, but I will cover your part on the program."

I missed the NACUA conference in Denver, only my fourth absence from a NACUA conference in the thirty-two years I had been involved in the association.

74

My time at Mayo Mallette has been the perfect end to my professional career. The partners, Cal, Pope, and now Paul, have been gracious about permitting me to teach most semesters, to be a frequent visiting speaker at classes on campus, to publish law review articles, and to speak at conferences sponsored by NACUA, Counsel of School Board Attorneys, Mississippi School Board Association, and Stetson Law School.

But one of the most delightful associations I gained from my time at the firm was with a four-legged friend.

One day, Diann Coleman and I drove to Cal's home to visit with his family. They were all outside when we arrived.

"Come see our new puppy!" one of the children urged. "He's in his pen!"

The children were beside themselves, but I noticed as we followed the children to where the puppy was penned that Cal's wife, Caroline, did not look happy. I overheard her talking to Cal as Diann and I played with the children and a precious black and white puppy.

"Cal, I cannot manage four children and this dog any longer. He's wild, undisciplined, and he needs time I don't have to give."

Cal looked at Caroline and me and suddenly grinned.

"Well, perhaps you won't have to," he said. Looking up at the heavens, he raised a finger. "Mary… Ann… Connell… ("MAC"). The puppy's name is Mac. I think divine intervention is here."

Somehow, twenty minutes later, Diann was holding the wigglesome, twenty-pound puppy in the passenger seat of her dark green truck while I backed the truck out of Cal's driveway.

"He won't ever grow to be much bigger," Cal assured us as we left.

Mac failed puppy kindergarten three times and grew to be seventy-five pounds.

But he has mellowed with age, minds well, and is now a joy of our life.

XI
A Reflection

75

My birth announcement — white smoke bellowing from the chimney on Park Street — was unusual and unexpected for Louisville, Mississippi, but so has been my life.

From the very beginning, my life's journey has not followed a traditional or expected pattern but has taken twists and turns I could never have anticipated.

As a child, I believed life would always be as happy and carefree as my first eight years. I was loved, cared for, and surrounded by family and friends who made me feel secure and at peace with the world. While I played kick-the-can, hide and seek, and attended birthday parties, life was uncluttered by worry. I wasn't aware of the impending world war. I had no way of knowing that my father would be absent for several years of my childhood. And, of course, my brother Billy's death was unthinkable.

My idyllic world disappeared on November 4, 1945. It was replaced by one filled with guilt and regret. And I compensated for those feelings by over-achieving. I believed, somehow, it might magically make up for my mistake.

As a child, I loved to go to the Winston County Courthouse to see my father try cases. He was articulate and prepared. He was courteous and yet a forceful advocate. He was an "Atticus Finch," representing mainly the poor, the injured, the forgotten, while at the same time serving as attorney for the board of supervisors and the Citizens Bank. On Sunday afternoons, he and my mother, his true partner and soul mate, and I rode around Louisville and Winston County, as he pointed out to us sites where his clients had been injured. My parents were my heroes. I knew from the time I was eight years old that my goal in life was to be as kind and loving and gracious as my mother and as good a lawyer as my father. The path to emulating my mother was open to me; the path to being a good lawyer was seldom open to a girl.

I was fortunate to grow up in a small town with excellent, demanding teachers and with enormous support in all that I did. Long before Hillary Clinton based her 1996 book on the ancient African proverb, "It takes a village to raise a child," my village of Louisville was doing just that for me. A wise school superintendent encouraged me, in 1954, to break the mold and run for student body president.

"You can do anything in this world you want to do," he told me, "if you are willing to work hard enough for it."

Ole Miss gave me a fine education. The wisdom of my professors enabled me to compete favorably in my careers. At the same time, I developed social skills and friendships for a lifetime. My time at Ole Miss also gave me opportunities to participate in a wide range of intellectual and cultural activities that have enriched my life. The university also introduced me to Dean Malcolm Guess and Helen Rhyne, who loved me and taught me to think on those things that are beautiful and meaningful in life, while turning a deaf ear to negativism and gossip.

Even though my path to law school was convoluted, that delay in fulfilling my dream of becoming a lawyer permitted me to turn to history and library science and obtain master's degrees in each field, which have both enriched my life.

Perhaps one of the most important learning and maturing experiences of my life was living in the Mississippi Delta, where I lived among people with money, both earned and inherited. That experience tempered my populism to a slight degree and taught me that there are good wealthy people, just as there are good poor people. And, then there was Money Luckett, who expanded my intellectual horizon tremendously and enlarged my capacity to love and share a beautiful, deep friendship.

Even though Bill was deeply hurt over the sale of the Rena Lara place, it turned out to be an unforeseen blessing. Our moving to Oxford in 1966 is the wisest move we ever made. Oxford is a cultural oasis in the state of Mississippi. Living in Oxford enabled me to return to school and to obtain that long-yearned-for law degree. I had the fortune of practicing law for five years with a fine group of fellow attorneys. That experience provided a valuable background to me for my years as attorney for the University of Mississippi.

My father's early death at age 57 in 1965 and Bill's untimely death at age 55 in 1982 were both major setbacks in life for me. I can think of nothing positive to say about either event, but with the help of family and friends, I weathered the storms and, thanks to my university attorney position, was able not only to provide financially for our children, but to have a superior quality of life.

The year I spent at the Harvard Law School was the most intellectually and spiritually fulfilling experience of my life. Since Harvard, I am a better lawyer and a better person.

The association with Mayo Mallette over the past thirteen and a half years has been an unforeseen lagniappe that I never thought would come my way. I feel the same gratefulness to still be teaching both school law and employment discrimination law and to have served as attorney for the Oxford School District for eight years.

One of the dominating themes of my life has been relationships – family, friendships, and professional. Because I lived most of my life as an only child, I always wanted someday to have a big family, preferably six boys. Instead, with some difficulty, I had four daughters and would not change it for the world.

I can always count on my oldest daughter, Elizabeth, and her husband, Lloyd, to welcome me into their home — and to with a willing spirit do anything I ever ask.

Stella Garrett Connell, my second daughter and a book industry professional, has spent the last year working on this story.

Mary Ann, my third daughter, and her husband, Roy Percy, are the parents of my twin grandsons, William Strong Percy ("Liam"), named for my father and Roy's father; and Phinizy Davis Percy ("Phin"), bearing an old Percy family name and the maiden name of Roy's mother, Davis.

My fourth daughter, Jane, was named for my Aunt Jane (my mother's sister) and given my mother's maiden name, Danzey. She and her husband, Mike, are the parents of my other two grandchildren — William Young Lee, named for Jane's father and grandfather and for Mike's father; and Mary Ann Lee, named for me and for Mike's mother, Mary Lee.

These four grandchildren have brought love, joy, happiness, and fun into my life. They call me Mimi, just as my children called my mother. My greatest pleasure is watching these four children play together so beautifully. They are all excellent students and sweet, caring people. William excels at baseball and reading; Mary Ann in all sports and reading. Liam is an artist and, as he puts it, "the fastest runner in my class." Phin is an excellent reader and an all-around good athlete. Liam and Phin are both taking piano lessons. They all love school and do well there.

Friendships took on an inordinate importance in my family's life because we did not have a large, extended family. Tragic events in my mother's young life separated her to a large degree from her siblings and her own parents. Other than my Strong grandparents, my Aunt Jane and Uncle Reuben, and my cousin Jane and her family, I did not have the family, the aunts, uncles, and cousins that many people enjoy. I adored my Aunt Elizabeth, my grandfather's sister, but did not know her husband, and she had no children.

I have been fortunate to have had many close friends, both men and women, who have remained with me over a lifetime.

The day my mother died, I sat by her bedside in my room on St. Andrews Circle in Oxford, when she said to me: "Mary Ann, have you called Mary Sharp Rayner today to ask about her mother's bad cold?"

"No, I am sorry to say, but I have not done that today."

"Listen to me Mary Ann," she said. "Go and call her now. You must always remember to nourish friendships every day, or someday they will not be there."

Each day I promise myself that I will be a better friend, more caring, more giving, more loving, but too often I let time, work, business keep me from doing those things that I ought to do.

In the words of the prayer of confession in the Episcopal Prayer Book, "We confess that we have sinned against you in thought, word, and deed, by what we have done, and by what we have left undone."

It is those sins of "omission" with which I am just as deeply plagued as those sins of "commission."

I hope that by telling my story — filled with both successes and failures, with those things I did well and those with which I did poorly — it will help someone else not give up on him or herself. My hope is that it will help them take each day that comes along as it unfolds.

I got nothing I asked for but all that I hoped for,
and I am among all people most richly blessed.

The Ole Miss Alumni Association Hall of Fame Awards Dinner, 2015

Epilogue

E. Grady Jolly calls me every year on my birthday. I am greeted with "Happy Birthday, Miss Eighth Grade."

The prayer I took from the First Baptist Church of Louisville in 1948 (which is printed in the front of the book) is still tucked away in my wallet. I read it regularly.

After **Mary Ann Mobley's** reign as Miss America, she embarked on a successful acting career, including two stints opposite Elvis Presley. She died in 2014.

George Fair practices law in Jackson, Mississippi.

Grady Tollison practices law in Oxford, Mississippi.

John Leslie served as mayor of Oxford for 24 years. He called me "The Sewer Queen" until his death in 2012.

The four law students I chastised in the back of the moot court room did amount to something. **Mike Mills** is a U.S. District Court judge. In 1995, **Ronnie Musgrove** was elected governor of Mississippi. **Roger Wicker** has served as a U.S. Senator since 2007. **John Grisham** is one of the world's bestselling authors.

Tommy Ethridge served as U.S. Attorney for the Northern District of Mississippi and as a professor of law at the University of Mississippi. He was the university attorney at Ole Miss until 1982. He lived in Oxford until his death on August 29, 2010.

My former student **Cooper Manning** still greets me with an earnest bow and says, "I'm praying, Mrs. Connell. I'm praying."

Chancellor Porter Fortune died in 1989.

Bill Battle's Collegiate Licensing Corporation manages branding for more than 200 universities representing $3.68 billion in retail revenues. Ole Miss was Battle's second client.

The **licensing program** at Ole Miss has generated more than $12.7 million in revenue for the university.

Since 1995, **R. Gerald Turner** has served as president of Southern Methodist University.

Tom Meredith served as president of Western Kentucky University, chancellor of the University of Alabama system, and commissioner of higher education for the Board of Trustees of State Institutions of Higher Learning. He and his wife, Susan, live in Oxford.

My Harvard Law School classmate **Barack Obama** served two terms as President of the United States.

After **Robert Khayat** retired as chancellor, he wrote an award-winning memoir, *The Education of a Lifetime*. He and his wife, Margaret, live in Oxford.

Warner Alford was athletics director at Ole Miss from 1978-1994. He served as executive director of the Ole Miss Alumni Associate from 2004-2008. He and his wife, Kay, live in Oxford.

Professor Kathleen Sullivan is a partner in the global litigation-only firm of Quinn Emanuel Urquhart & Sullivan in Los Angeles. She was professor of law and my thesis director at Harvard Law School. She served as dean of the Stanford Law School from 1993-2004.

Kathleen Santora is president and chief executive officer off the National Association of College and University Attorneys — a position she has held since 2001. She and her husband, Hugo, live in Annadale, Virginia.

Lee Tyner has served as university attorney since 2003. Lee is a past president of NACUA.

Cal Mayo, **Pope Mallette**, and **Paul Watkins** still practice law in Oxford.

My mother, **Danzey Strong**, and father, **Bill Strong**, are buried at Memorial Park Cemetery in Louisville, Mississippi. My brother, **Billy**, lies next to them. Upon the publication of this book, Billy would have been 76 years old.

My husband, **Bill Connell**, is buried at Oakridge Cemetery in Clarksdale.

My oldest daughter, **Elizabeth Sessums**, lives in Ridgeland, Mississippi, with her husband, Lloyd.

My daughter **Stella Connell** worked as a literary agent and book publicist for two decades. She now lives in Oxford and works for the business school at the University of Mississippi.

My daughter **Mary Ann Percy** lives in Oxford with her husband, **Roy** (my former law clerk who wore jeans to his initial interview with me). They have two children. Mary Ann is the staff attorney for the Circuit Court of Lafayette County. Roy is a federal magistrate judge for the U.S. District Court for the Northern District of Mississippi.

My youngest daughter, **Jane Lee**, lives in Brentwood, Tennessee, with her husband, Mike. They have two children. Jane is a loan specialist at Reliant Bank in Brentwood. Mike is a partner with Stinson & Lee Insurance.

At age thirteen, **Mac the dog** died peacefully with the professionalism, care, and compassion of Dr. Kathy Kvam on February 1, 2017.

I live in Oxford, Mississippi.

Acknowledgments

Two years ago, **Cal Mayo** stood in the hall outside the small conference room in our law firm and said to me: "I want you to write the story of your life, both personally and professionally, for your children and grandchildren. I think it will be interesting and helpful to them, as well as to younger women because in many ways you have been a trailblazer. Tell your story and write it not just to indulge in nostalgia but as an inspiration and encouragement to your grandchildren that they can do anything they want to do if they are willing to work for it."

That theme had permeated my life since Superintendent Elzie Heinz told me when I was in the 11th grade that I should run for president of the student body against two boys. I should not let the fact I was a girl hold me back. I thought Cal's idea was a good one.

That conversation started me on this voyage of delving into my past, reconnecting with old friends and colleagues, and starting on the journey to describe my "unforeseen life", a life I did not anticipate as a young woman but one that has given me nothing I asked for but everything I hoped for. I have been indeed most richly blessed.

Stella Connell is my second daughter. Without her guidance and assistance, I could never have written this book. She read every word I wrote over and over, correcting my errors of fact, doing independent research to help me fill in missing pieces of my life that I either did not know or had forgotten, and provided enormous help in editing. She has been a successful publicist with several New York publishing companies, but she rose to the occasion and helped me in an editorial realm.

She rearranged paragraphs, added sections I would probably have omitted, and suggested deleting parts that I thought were central to my story. We did not have a cross word in the process, even though I dreaded seeing her editorial marks all over what I thought were perfectly fine pages of manuscript. She always believed this book would be an encouragement for young women in whatever field they wanted to pursue.

Stella has the talent and creativity her father had in the artistic realm, one in which I am sadly lacking. I thank her for all the revisions she read, for her interest and support, and credit her with making this story, for whatever value it may have for others, come alive on the printed page.

Neil White is an author of a magnificent true story of confession and redemption, *In the Sanctuary of Outcasts*. He is also a respected editor and publisher, having published such works as Robert Khayat's *The Education of a Lifetime* and Dr. David Sansing's *Mississippi Governors: Soldiers, Statesmen,*

Scholars, Scoundrels. After talking with Stella and me about my story, he agreed to work with me on editing it for publication by Nautilus Press.

He is creative and meticulous with detail. He recognized early on that I was an over-achiever for a purpose and helped me explain why I have been driven all my life to succeed. With Neil's help, guidance, and patience, I hope we have created a narrative that tells a story of life-long guilt that directed my path in life.

I am sure he is exhausted with trying to write the lawyer out of me and help me create "scenes" instead of telling the story with one fact after another. For his guidance and assistance, I am grateful and appreciative.

To Neil's talented and dedicated staff, **Sinclair Rishel** and **Carroll Chiles Moore**, I thank them for their professional work done with a gracious and pleasant spirit.

I relied heavily on the scholarly book, *The University of Mississippi: A Sesquicentennial History*, **Dr. David Sansing** wrote in 1999 to celebrate the one hundred and fiftieth anniversary of the founding of the university. He covered in detail the events surrounding the election of John Hawkins as the first black cheerleader, his refusal to wave the Confederate flag, and resulting actions by Chancellor Fortune in iterating that the Confederate flag had never been and would not be in the future a recognized official symbol of the university. Dr. Sansing also wrote about the burning of the Phi Beta Sigma house and the Beta Theta Pi fraternity incident. Dr. Sansing graciously gave me permission to use his book without detailed footnotes. For his willingness to let me base my writing on this part of the university's history on his book, I am appreciative to this gentleman and scholar.

Sue Keiser is chief of staff to the chancellor. For 19 years, she has been the person who managed the chancellor's office and was privy to almost all events and documents that flowed through that office. She gave me access to all files of that office having to do with the 1986 and 1993-95 NCAA investigations, the Brewer trial, and the preparation of the application to shelter a chapter of Phi Beta Kappa. I could not have reconstructed many of those events without access to those files and the cooperation she gave me in using them.

No two people have contributed more to the University of Mississippi in so many ways than have **Mary Ann and Don Frugé**. They have both been generous with their time, energy, talents, and resources. From Don's 22 years of leadership of the university's development program and the University of Mississippi Foundation to Mary Ann's work with the Women's

Council, planning and overseeing the dedication of the Paris-Yates Chapel, they have supported programs, scholarships, and mentoring for many students. Both have assisted me in writing this book. I appreciate their interest in the project and long-years of personal friendship.

Liz Danford is a legal assistant at Mayo Mallette, who has provided hours of help to me in transposing this manuscript from WordPerfect to Word and transmitting it to Nautilus Publishing, always with patience and kindness.

Duke Goza was the first person I asked to read any part of this manuscript. He did so and advised me that I had included too much detailed discussion of law. His comment was later confirmed by the five readers who gave of their time and talent to reading the entire manuscript, including my law partner, Cal Mayo. While I told them all that they had mortally wounded me by saying that I had written far too much on the *Palsgraf v. Long Island Railroad* case, which I thought I had summarized in a fine fashion, I had to concede that every reader who agreed with Duke unanimously on this point must be right. So, I have condensed the great case to a mere mention. In the words of Cal Mayo, "if the reader is really interested in reading more about that case, they can Google it." I owe Duke appreciation for his reading and comments, but much more for years of a beautiful friendship.

To **William Lewis, Jr., Julia Thompson**, and the late **Becky Morton**, I express appreciation for the time and experiences they shared with me concerning the peaceful integration of the Oxford School District.

Dr. Jerry Jordan and **Jean Jordan** provided me with a detailed history of the University of Mississippi Concert Singers during the Jordan years, which is a story unto itself, but because of page limitations could not be incorporated into this book. That story of remarkable success will be preserved in the unedited edition of this work. For their gift of music to the world, I, and their many admirers, express appreciation.

To **Dr. Buddy Chain**, former president of the Oxford School District, my friend from college days, colleague from university working days, and my next-door neighbor, I thank him for the gift he gave me of the story he wrote of his life, *A Pleasant Journey: Some Recollections from Along Life's Way*.

To **Elise Winter** for her memoir of her days as first lady of Mississippi during the governorship of her husband former **Governor William Winter.**

Former Chancellor **Gerald Turner, Dr. Tom Meredith**, and **Dr. Les Wyatt** talked with me, read parts of this manuscript, and helped me refresh my memory of various significant events in the life of the university, for their willingness to take time out of their busy lives, I express my appreciation.

To Professor Emeritus **Dr. Max Williams**, the late **Emmett Marston**, the late **Professor Tom Mason**, **Dr. Mickey Smith**, as well as all members of the NCAA investigative committees, I owe a debt of gratitude for helping me recreate the facts and hours or hard work poured into defending the university through two investigations. **Langston Rogers** provided many details and data I needed, always with efficiency and cheerfulness.

To **Deck Fair**, who ran across a chapter on the NCAA while reading about the early days in Louisville and the four-generation friendship between our families and kindly suggested I write more about athletics.

Thanks to two former students, **Cooper Manning** and **Bill** \for verifying two stories I told about them from days when I taught each of them business law and for permission to use their names in this book.

Former **Chancellor Robert Khayat** and his wife, **Margaret**, have spent hours with me talking about the college days that Robert and I shared at Ole Miss, the friendship Margaret and I have shared through the years since we met when we both moved to Oxford, the history and important events in the life of the University of Mississippi, and the process of writing a story of my life.

Sandra Mayo, Yvonne Giffin McMillan, and **Julia Boren Baker** have all talked with me about life in Louisville, Mississippi, both in the past and in the present. For their assistance in helping me recall more clearly life in that special town, I thank them.

Dr. Ronald Schroeder did a superior job preparing the University of Mississippi Phi Beta Kappa faculty's application to shelter a chapter of the nation's most prestigious academic society. Dr. Schroeder generously let me use his files in writing this book and helped me recall details of our time working together on this project.

To **Lynette Johnson, Dr. Gloria Kellum, Warner Alford**, and all members of the Title IX Compliance Review Committee, I thank them for what they did to bring the University of Mississippi into much improved compliance with Title IX gender equity requirements and for giving me access to many of the documents we used in doing this work

To **Lee Tyner**, my valuable partner while representing the university, to **Donna Gurley** and **Rob Jolly**, associates in his office, and to **Margaret Sims, Mary Lou Owens**, and **Vicki Riter**, capable assistants in the office, I appreciate all you did for me through the years, as well as for retrieving files, and recollecting with me many of the incidents described in this book.

To **Bill Battle, Roger Lyles**, and **Kathy Tidwell** for their successful creation and management of the university's licensing program.

Thanks to **Kathleen Santora, Paul Parsons**, the staff, and membership of the National Association of College and University Attorneys for their many contributions over the years toward advancing the "effective practice of higher education attorneys for the benefit of the colleges and universities they serve."

Dr. Sparky Reardon shared with me his dissertation "Frank Moak's Legacy" and spent significant time with me recounting the history of student affairs at the university. I am grateful for his time, his memory, and his years of meaningful service to the University of Mississippi.

Grady Tollison, Dan Webb, and **Ronnie Roberts** provided me with valuable assistance in recalling the early days of practice together on the Square in Oxford, Mississippi.

Rick Burnham, my cousin Jane's son, gave me wise and helpful counsel in deciding what to include and what to omit from this manuscript. For his patience and wisdom, I express my appreciation. Rick also provided me with much information about my mother's family and the Self-Burnham families that I hope to set forth in an unedited version of this book.

Deep appreciation to **Milly West** for the beautiful tribute she wrote to Bill that was printed on the front page of *The Oxford Eagle* on the day of his funeral and for her permission to duplicate it in this book.

To **Diann Coleman** for her friendship, encouragement, and support, as well as her patience in listening to me tell the same stories over and over.

And to my readers **Mary Ann Frugé, Lucille and Ray Hume, Jon Levingston, Cal Mayo,** and **Margaret Love Denman**. I owe an enormous expression of appreciation to this group of highly intelligent, well-read friends who gave their time to read this manuscript and give me valuable feedback on how to make it better.

Many others provided information and assistance to me in wide-ranging areas, some of which I was unfortunately not able to incorporate into the book because of page limitations. I have saved them all and hope to have the complete, unedited manuscript bound for the university, Oxford, Louisville, and Clarksdale libraries, as well as any others who might be interested.

My gratitude extends to many others for their friendship and support through the years, as well as their interest in this project. I think each one knows how grateful I am and how much I cherish our relationships.

Mary Ann with her grandchildren, Mary Ann Lee,
Liam Percy, William Lee, and Phin Percy, 2015

BIBLIOGRAPHY

B. J. Smith Kelleghan with Annie Beth Smyth Davis, *I Built This House: The Story of Louisville's Oldest Buildings* (original sketches by Davis Love Fair, Jr.) (1976).

Woody Majure, *A Time That Was: Louisville 1939-1945*.

Nicholas W. Majure, *When the Woods Were Green* and *The Tallest Christmas Tree*, (1976).

Mary Karr, *The Art of Memoir* (Harper Collins 2015).

Bela J "Buddy" Chain, *A Pleasant Journey: Some Recollections From Along Life's Way*, (2013).

Elise Varner Winter, *Once in a Lifetime: Reflections of a Mississippi First Lady* (ed. By JoAnne Prichard Morris (University Press of Mississippi 2015).

Lee Smith, *Dimestore: A Writer's Life* (Algonquin Books 2016).

Robert Khayat, *The Education of a Lifetime* (Nautilus Press 2013)